D0897623

Ivy Compton-Burnett
A MEMOIR

Ivy Compton-Burnett

A MEMOIR

CICELY GREIG

GARNSTONE PRESS

IVY COMPTON–BURNETT · A MEMOIR
is published by
Garnstone Press Limited
59 Brompton Road, London SW3 IDS
ISBN: 0 85511 060 0

Printed by Butler & Tanner Ltd,
Frome and London

Contents

'I have a word to say . . .
Almost any character in any novel by I. C-B.

'What a difficult kind of work to choose!
But of course one did not
choose it. There was no choice.'
I. C-B., in a letter

Foreword

I have tried to give a portrait of the late Dame Ivy Compton-Burnett as I knew her during twenty-four years.

It all began some time in 1945 when the idea came to me to write to her and offer to type her next novel for her. Ivy took me at my word and brought me the manuscript of *Maidservant and Manservant* one day in March, 1946. I certainly had no intention of remaining her permanent typist: I had enjoyed her earlier novels and wanted to type one for the interest of reading the manuscript. But typing all that brilliance and wit fairly mesmerised me, and I remained her typist until she died in 1969.

A portrait of someone as unusual as Ivy must be of the 'warts and all' type. She was an autocrat – but never an arrogant one, and an intellectual. She was quite out of sympathy with our age. This made her formidable enough. But, together with those steely weapons of hers, weapons she knew how to use, were deeps of gentleness, kindness, humour and generosity. One might sometimes be petrified but one remained devoted.

There have been other books about this remarkable author, but as her typist I have my own word to say.

I have made brief commentaries on the work of Margaret Jourdain, which I typed during the years I knew her, because Ivy's devotion to Margaret was such that no one can write about the one without including the other. Margaret is forgotten now, but she should be remembered with her friend.

I

'Thank you for your card of a while ago. Can you type a novel for me without much delay? If so I will leave the MS at your address in a few days.'

The blue postcard was die-stamped with an address in the S.W.7 district of London. The date on it was 27 March 1946. The handwriting seemed at odds with the precision of the message, but this was only a first, quick impression, later corrected. It was a scrawling and sprawling hand, the letters large, wayward, and some of them – the capital B of the signature in particular – quirkily formed. The signature that sprawled across the card was I. Compton-Burnett.

This was the first of many cards and letters I was to receive from this most unusual and brilliant novelist. It was unexpected, and I read it with a leap of the heart. It was true I had written to her 'a while ago', as she put it, but my offer to type her books for her because I enjoyed reading them could hardly have persuaded her that I was efficient.

My while ago having been a matter of months, I stared at the signature with wonder and homage, fearful and unbelieving. My first impulse was to make contact without delay, before she changed her mind. There was no telephone number on the card, and her name was not in the Directory. Should I rush off to S.W.7, ring her doorbell, and cheerfully announce myself? No; out of the question. This author, I was sure, would expect a formal reply. And she had written that she would bring her manuscript to me if I was free to type her novel. I had only to write and tell her I was free, and she would come.

I remember writing in most careful English; no abbreviations, not my usual 'I'll be in and I'd be delighted to . . .'. With the image and the echoes of her characters and their speech, with the style of her stories and the shape of her sentences strongly in mind, I wrote 'I will be in . .' precise as a governess.

I had a vague image of the author herself, but looking at her hand-writing on the blue postcard, the image I had already formed of her remained. It was of someone quite formidable. And that was what she was, formidable in every way.

I first read about Ivy Compton-Burnett in 1936 or 1937. My father subscribed to the *New Statesman* and I always read the *Books in General* article which at that time was written by David Garnett. I have forgotten what books or book he was discussing that week, but I remember he wrote in a complaining way about the state of the novel at that time; there was not one, he said, to compare with *A House and its Head* by I. Compton-Burnett.

I had never heard of I. Compton-Burnett and I thought I knew about the more interesting and original writers of the day. It was a time when we were reading Virginia Woolf and Ronald Firbank and Aldous Huxley and Rose Macaulay and D. H. Lawrence, to mention my own favourites at that time. We had all become rather suspicious of 'fine writing', and Logan Pearsall-Smith wanted to bring it back, and wrote a pamphlet on the subject. We took note of rebels: we hailed Elizabeth Bowen as an outstanding rebel. I remember we said, in discussing her among ourselves that sometimes she wrote almost bad English, and we said it with a kind of rapture. It was the effect writers like Charles Morgan had on us, I suppose.

It was in this kind of climate that I saw the name I. Compton-Burnett for the first time, and I wondered why I had never heard of 'him' before, since I read book reviews and we were always interested in new writers.

When I went to Boots' Lending Library at Notting Hill Gate and asked for *A House and its Head*, it was produced for me as promptly as though I had asked for an Agatha Christie. At the same time I was reminded of a book, much in demand, that I was reading and I had to promise to return it the next day. That was why, when a friend called that evening, I was reading the book Boots wanted me to return, and the Compton-Burnett was lying unopened on the table.

'Of course you've read that,' I said, pushing it towards him.

He examined the book. Then he told me, to my relief, that he had never heard of the book and had never heard of the author. I showed him David Garnett's article. He assured me that if this author was as good as all that we would surely have heard of him. My friend also thought he knew the best writers of the day.

I told him he could take it to read, but I wanted it for the weekend. And I remember he flicked through the pages of *A House and its Head*.

'Oh, I'll read this easily in an evening,' he said. 'It appears to be written entirely in dialogue. Quite light I imagine.'

The next afternoon he brought it back. He threw it down on the table in a way that plainly showed me what he thought of it.

'Here's your Compton-Burnett,' he said. 'Definitely not my author. I couldn't get on at all with him. All the characters talk in the same way, a sort of pompous Victorian prose. And everything they say is very cynical.'

I was disappointed. When he had gone I opened the book. And I read:

'So the children are not down yet?' said Ellen Edgeworth.

Her husband gave her a glance, and turned his eyes towards the window.

'So the children are not down yet?' she said, on a note of question.

Mr Edgeworth put his finger down his collar, and settled his neck.

'So you are down first, Duncan?' said his wife, as though putting her observation in a more acceptable form.

Duncan returned his hand to his collar with a frown.

Duncan Edgeworth was a man of medium height and build, appearing both to others and himself to be tall. He had narrow, grey eyes, stiff, grey hair and beard, a solid aquiline face, young for his sixty-six years, and a stiff imperious bearing. His wife was a small, spare, sallow woman, a few years younger, with large, kind, prominent eyes, a long, thin, questioning nose, and a harried, innocent, somehow fulfilled expression.

The day was Christmas Day in the year eighteen eighty-five, and the room was the usual dining-room of an eighteenth century country house. The later additions to the room had honourable place, and every opportunity to dominate its character, and used the last in the powerful manner of objects of the Victorian age, seeming in so doing to rank themselves with their possessor.

'So you are down first of all, Duncan,' said Ellen, employing a note of propitiation, as if it would serve its purpose.

Her husband implied by lifting his shoulders that he could hardly deny it.

I read on, baffled but brave. And very soon I was enthralled. It is one of her great breakfast scenes, and the novel one of her finest. I read to the end, and turned back to the beginning, and read the book again. I renewed it at the library so often that at last the young woman suggested, kindly, that if I filled in the form pasted at the back of the book I would be able to buy it when it was withdrawn. So I filled in the form and some weeks later, when the book was withdrawn – I hoped for a new edition – I was notified. I paid two shillings and sixpence and the book was mine. A first edition of *A House and its Head* for half-a-crown.

Why did I like her books so much? I have been asked that question many times, sometimes with a note of incredulous exasperation. With Ivy one is either an addict or an abstainer. I became an addict from the first chapter of *A House and its Head*. Most of my friends, unfortunately, are abstainers. Suggest her, and if they have ever tried to read one of her books their reply can be an indignant refusal.

Her impact is powerful. Her sentences, strong, muscular and stark, carry such a weight of meaning that one's concentration is in thrall: one dare not miss a single word. Such a blast of wit, of intellect, of profound thought comes at one that at times the excitement is almost unbearable. This is mainly because the story is in dialogue, each character most sharply drawn, one finds oneself in sympathy with or hostile to the speakers.

C. P. Snow once wrote in a review of one of her novels that she asks too much of her readers. We must pay attention to the talk or we might forget who it is who is speaking; we must use our imagination and fill in areas of time and space that fall outside that rigid economy of hers. All this is true. But she remains the most rewarding writer of her time, the writer of the best English, a classic writer. Her sentences have the authentic music of a sentence from Cicero, they are cast in his mould, that perfect balance of synthesis and antithesis, comparison and contrast that Lyly, centuries later, was to turn into a game called Euphuism. Cicero's music is delightful wherever his influence lingers.

In prose, Dr Johnson can be majestically Ciceronian. In his Preface to his Dictionary, for example:

> I found our speech copious without order, and energetick without rules. Wherever I turned my view there was perplexity to be disentangled and confusion to be regulated.

Ivy's sentences have that authentic music. This one, for example, beginning *Brothers and Sisters*:

> Andrew Stace was accustomed to say, that no man had ever despised him, and no man had ever broken him in.

A typical Ivy sentence. Or this one, not eighteenth century but Elizabethan, spoken by Julia in *A Heritage and its History* on the subject of the proposed marriage between Hamish and Naomi:

'To tell you the truth, I have thought it might happen. To tell you more, I have hoped it would. To tell the whole, I should like it to do so now. It may be to say that I am a woman and a mother, but what is there against my being both? And what is there to prevent it? And why should I be any better if I were neither?'

There are sentences in Ivy's novels strongly Shakespearian, and there are passages in Shakespeare that can remind one at once of Ivy. This in *Henry IV*, part I, for example:

(Glendower says): 'I can call spirits from the vasty deep.'
(Hotspur answers): 'Why, so can I, or so can any man;
But will they come when you do call for them?'

A classical writer reflects every age of great literature. There are dramatic moments in the novels when she echoes the great rhythms of the Authorised Version. In *The Mighty and their Fall* for instance, when the fatally ill son, Ransome, returns to his mother, Selina, Ninian, the good son who stayed at home, says:

'You know I have married a wife . . . you will be a friend to her?'
'Yes, I know. And I have seen and heard. And I am her friend.'
Ransome sat down by Selina, and she heard him and understood. Her son had returned to her to leave her. He had numbered his days.'

As students we were told that there was no break in mood between Homer and Beowulf, the saga of the lone hero. Ivy was a Classics scholar. I was not taught Greek, but we had to study Beowulf, the stark utterances with their regular, strong beat of the Anglo-Saxon minstrels.

'Time passed on; the ship was on the waves, the boat beneath the cliff.'
'The slayer lay low, the dread earth dragon, reft of life, vanquished by violence.'

(I quote from Professor R. H. Gordon's translation of the Anglo-Saxon.)
'The cold held, bound the earth, could not break.' This is from *Manservant and Maidservant*.
A novelist who refuses to write in the idiom of her day appeals inevitably to a minority. When it is said of her books: 'People don't talk like that in real life,' the statement is true. Like Doughty, Ivy turned her back on the contemporary scene and related her art to a

centre of gravity removed from our time, to a more elegant and leisured age. Our manners, our Americanised speech were alien to her.

Born in 1884 she was, by birth and upbringing a Victorian–Edwardian, and she remained a Victorian–Edwardian. It was a way of life she knew, the only life she wanted to write about. In her novels her families live in country houses, and the head of the family is the local squire, though she does not use that word. Her own childhood was spent in Hove and her father was a doctor. He was twice married and had twelve children all told. Ivy was the eldest of the second batch, she had two younger brothers and two sisters. From what she told us her home life was very much like the life she describes in her novels. There were menservants and maidservants, family prayers, a schoolroom where a tutor taught the boys, a nursery for the little ones, and a nursemaid, Minnie, especially loved and remembered by Ivy. When she was twelve Ivy was sent to school and remained there for two years. Certain features of school life are faithfully observed in her novel *Two Worlds and their Ways*: the new girl's ordeal before the others – their sharp scrutiny of her clothes and of her mother's clothes, their curiosity about her home life, and those occasions of school life like the visiting day for parents and the school concert. She returns briefly to this scene in her last, unfinished novel *The Last and the First*.

After two years she continued her studies at home under her brother's tutor. She enjoyed Greek and Latin, normal subjects for young ladies at that time, and continued her classics studies at Royal Holloway College, Egham, where she got her degree. This College had been endowed soon after Ivy was born by Thomas Holloway a chemist who had made a fortune selling patent medicines, in particular an ointment that was to have an international reputation. He endowed a sanatorium for mental patients of the lower middle class, and a college for young ladies.

Ivy's first heroine, Dolores, also goes to a women's college and studies Classics, and she clearly had Holloway College in mind when she described Dolores arriving at the College, with a hundred other young ladies, and their introduction to the lecturers, to Miss Cliff, lecturer in English Literature and Miss Butler, who took Classics.

On the death of her father the family left Hove, a place Ivy disliked, and settled in Richmond. Her two brothers studied history at Cambridge, and Guy, the elder, died of pneumonia before the outbreak of war and while still an undergraduate. Her younger brother Noel got his degree and studied for a Fellowship at King's. He was a friend of Rupert Brooke and he and Ivy belonged to a set that included the Tennants and the Beresfords. Her two sisters, Vera and Julia, had had a musical training and shared a house with Myra Hess in St John's Wood.

Ivy's first novel *Dolores* was published in 1911. Her brother Noel had collaborated in it, but to what extent is uncertain. Ivy even declared that her brother 'meddled' with it, and in the last years of her life she used to say that she really could not remember who wrote what. I had learned by that time that she disliked talking about it: it was her juvenilia and she never included it in her list of published novels. I once mentioned it in a letter and was sharply reprimanded by return of post. Then I read the book and wished I had not. Her sister Vera once told me that at this time Ivy lived on a fairly concentrated diet of Victorian novels – in particular George Eliot. The book has strong echoes of Middlemarch, with Charlotte Brontë rumbling an accompaniment. Dolores, the heroine, is the dutiful daughter, setting duty before her personal wishes, duty to her father who wishes her to stay at home and teach the younger children – he is a country vicar – when she might accept a post at her college; duty to her friend who marries the man Dolores loves. It is all a dreadful warning to dutiful daughters, but that was not Ivy's intention then. After *Pastors and Masters* (1925) her outlook was altogether different. But by that time she was forty-one and had renounced her Christian teachings. There is a dutiful and an undutiful daughter in her last novel, *The Last and the First*, Madeline and Hermia. It is Hermia who gains a fortune and a husband, and Madeline stays dutifully at home. There is no doubt at all as to which one has Ivy's sympathy.

In 1911 the prose in *Dolores* would have been considered good. It was not a critical age. One of the characters in the book, an old lady of ninety-one, calls a man by his Christian name. The author says: 'It was one of her few evincements of greatness of age.'

There is much talk about religion in *Dolores*, and the conversation is altogether more objective than in the later novels. The problems of the day are discussed at social evenings, the question of forming a Temperance society – Ivy spells temperance with a capital letter – and the unification of churches, Church of England with Methodist and Wesleyan, and solemn warnings about 'Roman Catholicism, its spread and significance'.

When questioned about religion Ivy would say that she disliked the usual prayers and church services as a child, and gave it all up as soon as she became her own mistress. Dolores's uncle, the Dean, is described as being 'in the prime of his pomposity and portliness', but the two authors treat the vicars and non-conformist ministers in the book with gentleness. Ivy, the Latin scholar, pokes fun at the Minister who preaches on the text: 'In my Father's house are many mansions,' but it is gentle fun. The village doctor informs the minister later that the word mansion really means a resting-place. 'It is the Latin word *mansio* used by the translators of the Bible in its native significance,' he says. The Minister at once replies by protesting that it is surely better to stick 'to the old Gospel meanings', and the two talk at cross-purposes. It is one of the few amusing passages in the book, one that we recognise at once as Ivy's own.

Some months after her death I saw Ivy's proof copy of *Dolores* inscribed in her scrawling hand: 'To Noel Compton-Burnett from the Author.' Ivy obviously claimed authorship in 1911, but decided to blame her brother for most of it later.

The happiness of this early time in London came to an end with the outbreak of war in 1914. Noel, newly married to one of the Beresford girls, got his commission and was sent to France. He was killed in the Battle of the Somme in 1915.

When Ivy spoke of that time later, and of her two brothers, she always said their deaths quite 'smashed up' her life. This has been quoted of her in articles, and it is a phrase we most of us heard her use whenever she spoke of the war and the slaughter of her brother and his friends. It is a violent phrase, but Ivy was always very precise in her choice of words. Her pattern of life was indeed 'smashed up', to what extent one can only guess. She was an eligible and fairly well-off young woman, and she often told us that very many young women in her position were left unmarried because of the terrible death roll among the men of her generation.

It took her some years to restore the pattern of her life. She was very ill and she lost the urge to write. But the self-discipline that made her so remarkable a person, that unseen force in her that informed all her work, must have been strong even then. Ivy set herself the task of making tapestry chair seats, believing that the concentration and application necessary would stimulate the lost urge to write. I often spoke of those embroidered chair seats when we went into Ivy's dining-room at Braemar Mansions, and admired them, learning much later about their history.

During these years, the time between the publication of *Dolores* and the early war years, there was a tremendous upsurge of feminine activity, first under the leadership of Mrs Pankhurst and later, for patriotic reasons, when women put on uniforms and worked in hospitals and on farms, in barracks and overseas with the troops. Ivy remained aloof from the hubbub, mainly on account of her health, but also because public protest and turmoil were altogether alien to her nature. Many of her women are tyrants, but she is not concerned in her novels with women in public life. They remain in their homes, mostly, or rule as headmistresses. This is not to say that she was not interested in 'career women' – the opposite is true. It was her meeting with Margaret Jourdain soon after the end of the 1914 war that finally restored her, a meeting that was to result in a friendship of over thirty years.

But first to return to her meeting with me – an altogether different matter.

In 1946, when Ivy's first postcard came, I had given up the job I held during the war and returned to a freelance life. I could now and then write a short story for a woman's magazine, and I could type. A research student asked me to type a thesis for him, and though the subject was unfamiliar I found it interesting. I asked him to recommend me to other students. I had enjoyed typing a thesis, but unfortunately I found that students write other things besides their theses. The war had stimulated expression and students were writing poems and novels. I found myself typing very long novels in peculiar English. I decided to type only work that would be published – a high-handed policy that was not very profitable, but it gave me time for my own work. As this was not very profitable either, I decided to send cards out to one or two of the authors I liked reading, hoping one of them might be in need of a typist. One card certainly went to Ivy Compton-Burnett, c/o her publisher, another to Rose Macaulay. On the blank side of Ivy's card I wrote: 'I would love to type one of your novels. I have read *A House and its Head* seven times.'

Both statements were true. Some months later I received her card. By this time I had read all her published work with the exception of the early *Dolores* (1911) which I had not then heard about. I had dis-covered that she was a woman author – the I. Compton-Burnett on the title page had suggested a man. As she was by no means a popular author I had not seen a photograph of her, and before she came to my flat with the MS of her new novel I tried to imagine what the author of *A Family and a Fortune* and *Brothers and Sisters* was like. I saw her, in my imagination, as a mature and therefore a middle-aged woman with a vigorous and decided manner – (I thought of some of the fearsome women in *More Women than Men*) – someone sharply observant – I darted about my small sitting-room with a mop and a duster, and arranged the flowers and then, more carefully, to make a good impression, myself. I expected her to be a woman of few words, words of the commanding kind, perhaps a bit like those formidable women I had met during the war who had ended up as Colonels. Then I remembered how her books made me laugh, I remembered her wit and her children . . . was she someone gentle and quiet like Jane Austen? It was obvious from all her novels that, mentally, she belonged to the past. I had seen Rose Macaulay at a Book Exhibition and I decided, while I waited, that Rose and Ivy must be contemporaries.

When, quite punctually, the doorbell rang, and I flew to the door to open it, and we stood face to face, my first impression was of someone rather past middle-age. She said: 'Miss Greig?' and when I greeted her a small, grey-gloved hand jerked up to a receptive position, a movement that reminded me of my grandmother who had brought us up. She had the same way of jerking up her small, gloved hand on meeting someone, the fingers curled, as Ivy's were, so that one 'shook' – though that is not at all the word to use – only the fingers. It was an Edwardian way, and royalty's, politely formal, quite unlike our more vulgar and modern gripping and shaking habits.

I led her into the sitting-room, feeling tall beside her. She was quietly dressed with a dark grey coat and wore a draped kind of hat, both in very good taste. While we said trivial things about finding the way easily and my not being so far from South Kensington, I observed her closely. She was small and spare. Her features were good, and strong, the small nose aquiline, her complexion clear. Her manner and her talk were restrained, quiet, severe in a way. She wasted no words. She told me simply what she wanted, how she wanted it done. This may suggest briskness, but that is not at all the word to use of her. She was never brisk; she was always quiet. She had, I found more and more as I got to know her, a beautiful quietness about her. She listened more than she talked. As we sat together her quiet dignity interested me. She seemed to me quite an anachronism. I was used to people, it

18

seemed, who rushed about, arriving saying 'Oh Lord! I'm terribly late'. Ivy was the only person I knew who was never in a rush. When I say her manner was severe, I mean that it was plain she could be severe; there was a cold severity about her, even though, while we talked, her manner was calm and kind. She told me, in her rather weak voice, that she always wrote her books in pencil in school exercise books. 'The type-writing places pull the books apart,' she said. 'I think so that several girls can type at once and get it done with. But then they don't put the books together again.'

I promised her that I wouldn't tear her books apart.

My tortoiseshell cat, Prunella, had been sleeping unnoticed in a corner of the room. She now woke, sat up, and looked across at Ivy with her wide, golden stare. Perhaps she sensed some kind of witchery because she suddenly moved swiftly and quite silently towards us, and before I could stop her sprang on to Ivy's lap.

Ivy's reaction was immediate. With a twitch of something like horror she swept Pru off her lap. 'No,' she said. 'I don't like cats. I don't like them anywhere near me.'

Her manner was quite severe. I apologised at once and put Pru out.

'I like it to be plain that there is dialogue,' she went on smoothly, as I shut the door. 'Each character to have a different line.'

I nodded and tried to look reassuring. 'I know your work very well,' I said. 'I'm sure I shan't have any difficulty. And if I am stuck at all, perhaps I may ring you?'

She told me her number was under Jourdain in the book, and she gave it to me at the same time. I wrote it down. I had not then heard of Margaret Jourdain and thought it must be Ivy's husband.

This first meeting lasted barely ten minutes. It was strictly a business meeting, and Ivy made no attempt to move into a more friendly area of talk. She was cold and formal. She made no conversation, no friendly remarks, no looking about the room at flowers or pictures.

When she rose to go I asked her if she knew, about, how many words she had written in this novel.

She said: 'Oh, I've been asked that before, and I never know. I'm afraid I'm stupid about that kind of thing.'

I said it didn't matter. I would get on with it, I told her. But it might take about three weeks. I wasn't free the whole day.

She said that was all right. 'I hope it's long enough,' she added. 'If not, I shall have to write some more.'

Ivy was to say this every time she gave me the manuscript of a new book. It was a remark that largely explained her way of writing. Her plots unfold through a series of scenes in which the different members of the household, the elders in the dining-room, the children in the school-room, and the servants in the servants' hall, express themselves, in their sharply contrasted and individual ways, commenting on the predica-ment they find themselves, or others in. Ivy liked to say, in interviews with the press, that her books are something between novels and plays. When I typed *Manservant and Maidservant* I was often reminded of that remark of hers, and of the one she made to me about writing some more if necessary. Mortimer's conversations with Bullivant are in the form of interludes in the development of the plot, interludes for commentary, commentary that accepts whatever may befall, as in a Greek chorus, sharpening the edge of shadows, probing deeper into the meaning of life. These passages hold many of the best things to be found in her novels, and I believe she enjoyed writing them, when the plot stands still and two characters try to find its meaning, or relate it to the general human predicament. And it was her way of filling the book out without padding. Ivy was never guilty of padding, and was always critical of those writers who were.

But on that morning in March 1946 I had not yet opened her parcel with the manuscript of her novel. We said goodbye to each other at the front door, and I flew back to the sitting-room. When I opened the parcel I found fourteen school exercise books of the cheaper kind, blue paper covers and multiplication tables on the back cover. I remember thinking this last detail quite a fitting decoration for a book of Ivy's. Her books so often have a sort of inexorable logic about them, like twice one is two.

Each exercise book bore the title *Manservant and Maidservant* and each book was numbered. This was as well because in writing she went smoothly on from one book to another, beginning a sentence on the last line of book one and finishing it on the first line of book two. Chaos could have come about if the books had not been numbered; a difficulty I had with her last, unfinished novel with its loose pages torn out of the exercise book, and the pages unnumbered. But that was written when Ivy was old and weary. Normally her manuscripts were neat and clear. Her novels were always written in pencil, but my first examination of her manuscript in 1946 surprised me: this pencilled writing was not at all the sprawling hand with the large, looped letters that I had seen on her postcard. This pencilled writing was careful and neat, with small, close letters and every word quite easy to read. She wrote only on the right-hand page, leaving the left-hand page for additions and corrections. It was a marvel to me that Ivy could have written so many novels in pencil, something I can use only for short messages or shopping lists. She rubbed out on every page, and sometimes the whole page was rubbed out, but she wrote over the rubbed-out part, and managed to do so quite clearly and neatly. She used her pages with economy, leaving no margin.

These exercise books that were to come into my hands every eighteen months or so until 1963 were a delight to me, and I used to examine them as one might the Dead Sea Scrolls. There is a word *palimpsest* which I came across about this time. It is from a Greek word meaning 'scraped again'. It is a noun, or rather what the dictionary calls a substantive, and in this case refers to 'paper or parchment prepared for writing on and wiping out, like a slate' – all rather Ivy-sounding. I always thought of the word when I read her novels in manuscript.

In a limited way Ivy and I were both keen gardeners. She had a long balcony, I had a ground floor flat and later, when I moved to the country, a fairly large garden. Ivy was strict about dead-heading, weeding, watering and general tidying-up. All had to be done regularly. She disliked disorder.

I mention this because when, later, I was to know her flat well, and her balcony garden, and those most precious blue exercise books, I learnt from them how certain words can become as invasive as weeds. Her perennial, and one as troublesome to her (and now to me, the only quirk I inherit from her) as speedwell or buttercup in a garden was the word *that*. The word occurred in her sentences and was crossed out on almost every page. I can only give examples from her last novel, unfinished at the time of her death, but much of it gone over in her careful way. This novel was written during the last years of her life, and she had not finished it, nor her revision of it when she died, two months after her eighty-fifth birthday. But the discipline is there on every page she revised.

Overleaf are three sentences all written originally with the word *that* in them.

'It is nothing that you would understand.'
'You know what I have asked for, and you know that I will have it.'
'We must see that you don't have too much of it.'

All three *thats* are crossed out

But sometimes, having crossed out her *that*, she re-wrote it. Here is a passage where both *thats* were crossed out, but in a later revision she restored the first.

'Mater has found us a greater trial in her life than we knew.
'It does not mean that we have found her any less of one.'
'I suppose we should remember that she had to bring us up.'

She disliked our outworn words and phrases. She might use them in conversation, and she wrote them in her manuscripts. But she crossed them out in revision. The *of course* in the following sentence has a line through it, and so has the first *that*.

'It does suggest that there is something about you that we missed in our family life. Though of course that may hardly be the sphere for it.'

Vague words are crossed out. In this sentence *somehow* is crossed out.

'Hermia had a look of being somehow unusual.'

In place of *somehow* Ivy wrote *personally*, a stronger word, and more typical of Ivy. She had a precise and exact mind. She was familiar with our modern talk, our idioms, our way of working words to death – words like basically, for instance. She read the novels of her contemporaries, English and American, and we often discussed them. Sometimes a word like *impact* occurs in her writing, another well-worn word of our time. The word comes in her last book and she has crossed it out and used the word *impression* in its place. Her revision of the following sentences shows how she can use words as we lesser mortals use them, but in revision she crosses them out.

'To someone who was *actually* a stranger . . .'
'The large school in town *that* is not doing *too* well.'

The words in italics were rejected.

Her sentences have a distinctive lilt to them. When a word occurs out of tune, as it were, it is crossed out.

'My grandmother was never to lift *up* her head again.'
'We know *very* little as yet,' said Sir Robert.
'There seems *to be* no room for doubt.'
'And *it is* not only powers *that* are in question,' said Eliza.

The words in italics are all crossed out.

She corrected me when I, unconsciously, corrected her. I typed *judgment* because that is how I write it.

'I like the *e*,' Ivy said, in her quiet way.

I always thought she used commas rather freely. I left some of them out, thinking they could not all have been meant. With a pencilled manuscript, and one with many rubbings-out and corrections, one gave oneself the benefit of the doubt. But Ivy rescued them all. I left commas out in *Manservant and Maidservant* (before I knew better) and heard no more until her next manuscript was in my hands. There was one of her little notes:

'Do not leave out any commas. They are all necessary.'

However, on that morning in March 1946 my first concern was to read. Did this novel open with a breakfast scene?

On opening the first exercise book I found a note, to me, written in pencil and signed. It was written on the back of a Christmas card that bore a printed greeting:

With all good wishes for Christmas
and the New Year from
Lady Clapham.

I turned quickly from Lady Clapham's message to Ivy's. I read:

Please do it all yourself.
   „   do not take books to pieces.
   „   leave spelling and stops, except in cases of obvious slips.
   „   finish it as soon as you conveniently can, giving careful work.
   „   Carbon copy.
My pages have varying numbers of words. Best to reckon by your own.
Please put fasteners near enough to edge, to leave MS flat for corrections.

Ivy Compton-Burnett.

This was digested by me in about a second, and carefully filed. Then I read the opening of the novel.

'Is that fire smoking?' said Horace Lamb.

'Yes, it appears to be, my dear boy.'

'I am not asking what it appears to be doing. I asked if it was smoking.'

'Appearances are not held to be a clue to the truth,' said his cousin. 'But we seem to have no other.'

Horace advanced into the room as though his attention were withdrawn from his surroundings.

'Good morning,' he said, in a preoccupied tone, that changed as his eyes resumed their direction. 'It does seem that the fire is smoking.'

'It is in the stage when smoke is produced. So it is hard to see what it can do.'

'Did you really not understand me?'

'Yes, yes, my dear boy. It is giving out some smoke. We must say that it is.'

Three weeks later I had finished typing the novel. Ivy had asked for one carbon copy. 'Curtis Brown wants it. I don't know what for. I think to send to America,' she told me.

There was never any difficulty in the typing of her manuscript, except in the case of her last unfinished novel with its many loose pages. Later, I had to keep an eye on the names she chose for her characters. In her last novel Mrs Dunn becomes Mrs Duff, and Amy becomes Mabel, both names changed halfway through the book. This also happened with a name in *A God and his Gifts*, written in 1962–3, her last finished novel. But this was a small detail. Critics have talked about a falling off as she grew older, and I think there was in her plots. But her writing never changed. And her wit remained sharp, the knock of her sentences as powerful, the same strong beat and rhythm throughout. And the pleasure I got from typing those sentences can't be put into words. Their beauty slowed me down. I would read the sentence I had just typed again, and stare at the finished page. There they were, beautifully shaped and rhythmical. I looked for them with every fresh manuscript and I was never disappointed. I remember writing to Ivy about this some years later. I wrote about a novelist we both liked whose style, always interesting and adventurous, was becoming positively peculiar. Or so I thought. I wrote that I was thankful she never let us down, and I quoted Virginia Woolf's Bonamy: 'I like sentences that don't budge though armies cross them. I like words to be hard.'

When Ivy was asked in interviews if she had a favourite among her novels she always named *Manservant and Maidservant* as her favourite, and with it *A House and its Head* – 'two-thirds of it'. *Manservant and Maidservant* was the novel she particularly enjoyed writing, though this enjoyment, she was to say, 'was not in any strong sense'.

It is a novel of tremendous vitality and, I think, shows us the author

24

at the height of her powers. Her enjoyment in her characters, Bullivant and Mortimer, Gertrude and Cook and Miss Buchanan, Nurse and the children, spills over, as it were. Like Dickens she magnifies their faults and virtues and peculiarities; unlike him she stops short of caricature. She is concerned with the dignity of the individual: this is obvious in every novel. In *Manservant and Maidservant* Gertrude almost loses hers, but she manages to save it, indeed she emerges from the final scene almost triumphantly.

> '. . . And now I must hasten home, leaving only happiness behind, and so glad to leave it.'

There is comedy, high comedy, in this novel, and near tragedy. It is a good example of her gift for being able to change the tone and tempo of her story just when everything has been working up to a fortissimo. There comes an uneasy calm, a feeling of bewildering anti-climax; her characters stand, dazed and amazed, like people in a Greek tragedy, wondering what next will befall them. But the old tune starts up again, each one goes on more or less as before. It all seems to be inevitable, and the good and the gentle submit once more to the tyrant – and there is always a tyrant in Ivy's novels – but he has become less of a tyrant because, simply, he sees himself as secure. This is one of her sharpest breaks with tradition, that the less scrupulous of her characters usually come off best at the end of the book. And the good are re-signed, being what they are. For this she has been called a cynic, but cynicism is something she enjoyed and made enjoyable. And like Shakespeare, like Virginia Woolf, she never puts people into separate compartments of good and evil. As Terence says in *Elders and Betters*:

> 'We are very unfair to criminals. They only make one blunder out of so many. They ought nearly always to have the credit of the crime. What right have we to be so exacting, when we are only criminals at heart?'

One of the great beauties of *Manservant and Maidservant* for me are the chorus-like exchanges between Mortimer and the butler Bullivant. When Ivy told me 'If the book is not long enough I must write some more', these exchanges were the interpolations she allowed herself, rather than any other padding. Interpolations is a pompous-sounding word, but it is Ivy's word – she used it to me, and she always chose her words carefully. The *Oxford Dictionary* defines the word *interpolate* as: *to alter or enlarge a book or writing by insertion of new matter.*

Ivy's interpolations are the poems in this book, with the strophe and anti-strophe of a Greek chorus. Here is Mortimer asking Bullivant about his mother.

'Were you afraid of yours?'

'I would never open my mouth against her, sir.'

'Do you feel that she can hear you?'

'There are things beyond us, sir.'

'Do you expect to be re-united?'

'Well, sir, I would not be definite; united perhaps being hardly the word in the first place. But anything derogatory applies only to myself.'

'Do you wish you had been a better son?'

'Well, there are things in all our hearts, sir. Not that I ever forgot that she was a woman. It was only that I was confronted with other things.'

'Will you think of it on your deathbed?'

'That will be rather late in the day, sir.'

'It might be thought to be the right moment.'

'Well, in that case, sir, it may be put into my mind. But I shall not go to seek it. Making my peace at the last moment is hardly in my line. And my mother would have condemned it. That was her tendency, sir. Indeed the whole thing was that her standard was too high. In one sense I could not have had a better mother.'

When the typing of *Manservant and Maidservant* was done, and the pages bound and covered, I telephoned Ivy. I wanted her to ask me to bring the typescript to her house, my curiosity now aroused as to her setting and family.

'I have to go out,' she told me. 'And I shall be in your direction.'

We fixed a time for the next morning. And the next morning I put the top copy on the table and her chair in front of it, and I waited with a fluttering heart.

She gave me her quiet greeting, and when we reached the sitting-room she walked at once to the table and sat down and opened the copy and began to read the first page without saying a word. But in about a minute she said: 'This is very nice.'

Then she turned to the last page of all and read the last paragraph and said again: 'This is very nice. Thank you so much.'

I told her how much I had enjoyed typing it. 'Typing can be such a slog, sometimes. This was marvellous to do.'

There followed a silence, and these silences between us I was to experience very often, at lunch, at tea, with sherry, or just sitting before her fire chewing chocolates with her. One might think from her books that Ivy was a good conversationalist. She could not be called that. She was more a good listener. She was hospitable, she loved her tea parties with her friends all talking round her, but she herself was 'a sealed fountain' – the phrase is Edward Gosse's – interested, courteous, putting in her word, the still centre. Sometimes we were five or six round her table at tea, and one or two led the talk and kept it going at a fairly cracking pace, with the rest of us flinging in a word now and then, and Ivy often doing no more than that, though she always followed every word with close attention. She loved vivacious talk. She once told me how she loved to hear Rose Macaulay and Ernest Thesiger together, when Rose 'seemed to bubble over with high spirits'.

When I knew her much better I understood her silences, but I suppose in 1946 I was a fairly conventional young woman and I found her silence awkward. We sat together with her manuscript and the typescript of her new book between us and she waited for me to say something. A question hung in the air: 'Having typed the book, what did I think of it?' But Ivy never asked me that question, and though I was often to write to her with almost excited enthusiasm about her books, we seldom talked about her work together. I never had the slightest doubt that she was one of our best writers, but adulation is not at all a matter for conversation.

To break the silence I said cheerfully: 'Well, now I wonder what the critics will have to say.'

Hardly a brilliant remark and one that Ivy digested in silence. I kept my peace too. I had the carbon copy before me and busied myself with its fasteners to cover my confusion.

But Ivy kept me on the hook. She looked at me directly and said: 'I think it's a story with a good straightforward plot, don't you?'

That was easy to answer. I agreed at once. I said again, with warm emphasis: 'Oh, I enjoyed it tremendously. I'm so looking forward to reading it again.'

Trite and perhaps polite-seeming, but I had done my best. She heard me in silence, said nothing, seeming to wait for more. But I gave up. I was Cordelia-dumb. And Shakespeare was right. One must heave one's heart into one's mouth and make a speech when it's expected of one. Not to do so brings disappointment and confusion. Ivy was disappointed, and I was confused. And face to face with a writer whose every sentence is a delight, what words could I use? We were different generations, we were strangers, and now there was a wide, cold gulf between us.

I turned stiffly to practical matters. I had not been able to get a suitable cover for the carbon copy. Our local branch of Rymans was out of them – this was just after the war, it must be remembered, when there was still an acute shortage of paper.

'May I bring it along in a day or two?' I asked her. 'I shall have to try some places in the City.'

Ivy agreed. She told me where she lived, giving me very clear directions to Cornwall Gardens. Then she put the top copy and her manuscript into a bag she carried, and our interview was over.

The next morning she telephoned. After all, she would rather have both copies at once as she wanted to start correcting, and it was easier to work on both copies together.

'Can't you bind it with something you've got?' she asked – a typical Ivy remark. She was vague about all practical matters, vague to the point of helplessness. I promised to call at her house in about an hour. I had, in fact, found a cover and the carbon copy was quite ready for her. I pushed it into a paper bag that had once held a new hat and hurried out, almost running up the hill from my flat in Holland Park Avenue to Notting Hill Gate.

This was the first of many journeys to Braemar Mansions. A bus took me to Palace Gate, then one had a short walk down to the Gloucester Road. The houses and shops were to become familiar, Millais' great house on the left where Effie once held court, and the beautiful old houses along Palace Gate mixing, as the years passed, with more modern ones. Then came the bustle of Gloucester Road where Ivy did her shopping: a shop on the right sold home-made cakes and I often bought one on my way back from Ivy's flat to take home. There was a shop that sold flowers and fruit and vegetables, where later I bought flowers for Ivy – and how she loved flowers! There was a second-hand book shop where I found a copy of Henry James's last and unfinished novel *The Ivory Tower*. Ernest Thesiger lived in a block of flats just before one turned into Cornwall Gardens. Here the houses were rather drab, the gardens dreary with London-coloured shrubs. Braemar Mansions was on the gardens' side at the end of the road, and there was a pillar-box at the corner of the flats where I posted Ivy's letters for her when I came away. Braemar Mansions consisted of two houses, the front door of one was blocked and bore a notice to use the further door. This accounted for the size and spaciousness of the flats – Ivy's stretched right across the two buildings. It was a small corner of London that for many years remained the same, quiet, and aloof from the bustle and change of the contemporary scene. It was the right setting for Ivy. Braemar Mansions was to seem a mysterious place to me, the six flats all occupied, the inhabitants always invisible. The small hall was dark. There was an IN and OUT board with tenants' names, and I. Compton-Burnett was always marked IN. There was a lift, but one went up a short flight of stairs to the first floor landing with a front door on the left and right of the landing. Ivy's was on the left, and the door bore the notice *Please Knock and Ring*. I knocked and pressed a button which put a light on over the door. By the time I had found and pressed the right button the maid was already opening the door, and I was flustered and apologetic.

The maid, I learned later, was a cook-housekeeper-maid. There were to be different ones down the years, and one saw a gradual change in their appearance. The first one was properly starched and formal, disciplined and silent, answering only when spoken to. Later ones greeted one by name with a smile, said what a day it had been, relaxed and talkative in their nylon and coloured overalls.

On this, my very first visit, I hardly set foot in the flat. Both ladies, I was told, were out. Yes, Miss Compton-Burnett was expecting me to leave a parcel. I handed the carbon copy over, and left.

I walked away rather sadly. Next year the book would be published. And the year after that, if Ivy's rate of production remained the same, there would be another novel. But it seemed a long time to wait. I had no idea as to the other lady the maid referred to, but I was soon to know.

A few days after my journey to Braemar Mansions I received by post a bulging envelope that, when I opened, I found to be full of old bills, circulars, half-sheets of letters and opened out envelopes, all scribbled over and loosely pinned together. Hunting about all this waste-paper for a clue, I came on a headed post-card and saw, with a leap of interest, that it bore Ivy's address. There was a message to me asking if I would kindly type the enclosed article. It was for *Country Life* and the writer would like it fairly soon. The signature was Margaret Jourdain.

I had not then heard of Margaret Jourdain the writer, who, by this time, was an acknowledged authority on English furniture and decoration, and the author of two books on the subject: *English Interiors in Smaller Houses* (1923), and *Regency Furniture* (1934). She had also written books on English furniture in collaboration with others. During the five years I knew her she wrote mostly articles for *Country Life, Apollo* and *The Connoisseur*, and one book, *The Work of William Kent*, published in 1948.

Typing a manuscript for Ivy was a delight: typing from Margaret's scribbled notes written on odds and ends of scraps from the waste-paper basket was no delight at all. I learned very little of her subject from them; they read like those brief notes one makes in a Reference Library. The task could have been irksome if it hadn't also seemed so ludicrous to be reading a note about the treasures of a stately home on the back of a bill for coal. I used to sift through the scraps, reading both sides with equal care, the circulars, the old Christmas cards, and the letters. I remember one was from Osbert Sitwell asking Ivy to join some writers' society. As Margaret's writing was slovenly I made many mistakes and there were many corrections on my typed pages. But when, later, I gave these to Margaret and apologised for my mistakes, adding that I found her writing difficult, she said, with her attractive drawl: 'Oh, but it doesn't matter at all. It's only for a publisher.'

After her death in 1951 I re-read these articles and the one book I had typed for her. Margaret was no stylist; she could hardly be called a writer, except that that was what she did. She was concerned with facts and these were the fruit of a great deal of research, so much, in fact, that at least two or three footnotes were necessary for every paragraph. These give us the references of the many quotations and letters from contemporary sources. Margaret was generous with quotations so that in spite of what reviewers called 'her bleak style' the material was full of interest. This is especially true of her book on William Kent and the chapter devoted to his work as a landscape gardener. His contemporaries had grown tired of the formal Elizabethan garden. 'Is there anything more shocking than a stiff regular garden?' one of them asks – (but no footnotes from me: Margaret's books can be had from the libraries). They were outspoken, these friends of Kent, and he came in for a certain amount of criticism himself. He liked to break up great stretches of lawn, for instance, by 'striking a dozen trees here and there' – so that 'a lawn looked like the ten of spades' they said. But Kent's flair, perhaps, was in his use of water. He liked water, a great sheet of it at the end of a vista or, if that would not do, 'a stream that serpentizes' – my favourite of Margaret's quotations. She goes on to tell us that Kent set the fashion for 'serpentining' streams, but the landscape gardener who designed Hyde Park disliked the fashion which is why our Serpentine serpentises so little.

I wondered later if Ivy ever lent a hand in putting Margaret's notes into book form. Certainly the sentences are not Ivy's. I remember I made nothing of an article I typed for Margaret under the heading *Royal Stuart Embroideries of the Sixteenth Century* until I read it later in *The Connoisseur* of June 1949. Printing and editing and generous illustrations had worked their transformation, and I was enchanted by the article. There were the same factual sentences, and there were many footnotes. But the theme was tragic. It told how Mary, Queen of Scots, filled in some of her long hours of imprisonment by embroidering her bed-curtains and covers. Her patterns were taken from those Emblem Books that were so popular at that time, and Mary's choice of Emblems – symbolic, crestlike pictures with their accompanying mottoes – reveal her hopes and fears at a time when she and her friends were scheming for her freedom. Birds in flight, horses, a phoenix rising from the flames, and consoling mottoes: 'Sorrows pass and Hope abides,' were stitched in bright colours on her bed covers.

Ivy once, to my certain knowledge, wrote a short piece over Margaret's name, but unfortunately I have not yet been able to find it. It was written in answer to a critic who had given a rather poor account of a book by Margaret, I think her book on Kent. It appeared in one of the journals that notice such books, and I happened to pick up the following number in some library. Margaret's answer, a short paragraph, appeared in it, but it had been written by Ivy. I had not the slightest doubt of it. The sentences were like hammer blows. Margaret could not have written them. This was in 1949, and I still hope to find what I believe is the only piece of writing of Ivy's in print outside her novels. She always refused to write articles or reviews, saying that novel writing was the only form of writing she cared about. But it was typical of her to come to the defence of her friend like this.

The two women, Ivy and Margaret Jourdain, were as close in spirit, as mutually sympathetic, and as devoted, each to the other, as two friends could be. To a third person they were unlike in every way. Ivy was small and spare, and had a rather tight, neat appearance. She always wore long, black dresses with a white edging at the neck, and these black clothes seemed not to change, summer or winter. In very cold weather she wore little velvet jackets – there was a pink velvet one I liked especially. Such things as cardigans or sweaters were not in her world.

Margaret was heavier in build, and her clothes, which were very good and in a style of her own period – I am not quite certain which – had a draped look. I remember seeing her once in the Library of the Victoria and Albert Museum. She rustled and flowed between the bookshelves, a harmony of soft pinks and greys and E flat, so that heads were turned.

In manner, too, they were quite different. Ivy had a strict, almost schoolmistressy manner, but Margaret was languorous-seeming, with a charming graciousness. Ivy's voice was weak, Margaret's had a good, full tone; she spoke with a cultured drawl that was very attractive.

Both had their hair folded away in a band. Ivy's was always tucked in neatly, but Margaret's hair, which was fairer, was less disciplined and had a look of having been pushed under the band here and there in a haphazard fashion. I always disliked Ivy's head-band. One had no idea as to her brow – whether it was wide or high or low, because the band stayed firmly just above her eyebrows.

Margaret had a kindness of manner that Ivy seemed to lack. She was certainly not without kindness, but her wall of reserve was formidable, her dignity impregnable – interviewers always spoke of 'her iron dignity'. Her mask of strictness had a subduing rather than an encouraging effect. She could be awesome, many felt awe in her presence and said so. I felt a certain coldness in those early years; she had beautiful manners but she could correct one sharply and Margaret, who had an altogether warmer manner, would rush in quickly with some soothing remark. Perhaps Ivy thought I should have the wits to counter a rebuke, but I never had any wits, alas, in Ivy's presence. When I first knew her I had to struggle against an overmastering shyness. I felt at ease with Margaret always, hardly ever with Ivy.

Between the typing of *Manservant and Maidservant* and the typing of her next novel *Two Worlds and their Ways*, I was working fairly regularly for Margaret and I was often at the flat for tea. In those days tea at Braemar Mansions was something of an ordeal and different in every way from the tea-parties I so much enjoyed later. I remember very well my first tea there, and my extreme nervousness.

The flat was a large one, and one followed the maid down a fairly long passage to the door of the sitting-room. One was announced and always most graciously received.

This room which I came to know so well, was 'large and light and chill, and furnished with few and stately things . . . good to look at, less good to live in'. I quote from *Manservant and Maidservant*. One wall was taken up with two large French windows, floor to ceiling high and opening on to the balcony. This balcony was Ivy's joy, it extended along two walls of the flat and one could walk on to it from the bed-rooms or kitchen as well as from the sitting-room. The balcony railing held a trough and this was Ivy's garden, and always gay with flowers from spring to autumn. On this first visit there were petunias in bloom. I thought they were flowers that needed less water than most flowers, and said so. Ivy corrected me. They had to be watered twice a day. Later I became more involved with Ivy's garden, but on this first day I was more interested in the room and its furniture.

There was a beautiful eighteenth-century bookcase on the left of the door. I saw in it a set of Jane Austen, and a set of Shakespeare, books by Fielding and Sterne, the *Dialogues* of Plato, Plato's *Republic* and a volume of Sophocles. I always regret that I never talked to Ivy about Plato. As a student I had to read the *Dialogues* and the *Republic* and I still have copies of my favourites – the *Phaedo* and the *Symposium*. I had to read them in Jowett's translation. Ivy, of course, had studied them in the original. I was a reader, she was a scholar and I think I had an inferiority complex. Ivy loved Jane Austen – she put *Pride and Prejudice* first, but I preferred *Emma*. I liked Henry James, Ivy had read one or two of his books and had no great liking for him. He was not one of her authors.

One expected more books, but really there were very few. Later, however, as Ivy became better-known, especially among contemporary novelists, there were always the newly-published books of friends lying about. Ivy would pick up the book and say: 'So-and-So has sent me his latest novel. Have you read it?' There were always some on a table in the hall, and on the table in the sitting-room.

The fireplace was opposite the door and there was a small, and very beautiful little bureau, of the Davenport kind, on the right of the fireplace. This was Ivy's desk, and I imagined her sitting there writing her novels until she told me she always wrote her books 'sitting in one or other of the two armchairs', and never sitting at the desk. These armchairs were on each side of the fireplace, and the sofa between them formed a set, and the three pieces were covered with the same material which for many years, certainly during the last years of her life, was black. Beautiful period chairs, two or three of them Hepplewhite, stood against the wall, and there were Hepplewhite chairs in the dining-room. The curtains at the huge windows were of rose-coloured silk; they were very old, worn and even torn in places. Later, these were changed. A table stood between the two windows, and this was laid for tea.

We sat and talked before the maid brought in the tea-pot. I admired the fireplace which I could see, from the urn and the scrolls, was Adam. Margaret said they had it in the flat at Linden Gardens and had decided to bring it with them.

'We wished we had left it,' Ivy said. 'They had to knock the wall down, almost, there, to bring it here, and then almost knock the wall down to install it here and remove the other one. It was an expensive business.'

It was a collector's room, a room one could talk about. The two small, elegant fire screens on their tall stands which stood against the wall facing the window, an armed Hepplewhite chair between them, were later to appear in more than one photograph of Ivy. There was only one picture in the room, a rare Japanese mirror painting in an exquisite blue. Margaret was later to write on these paintings.

When the maid put the tea-pot and hot water on the table Ivy pulled a chair out for me, and I looked at it for a moment with interest. By now Margaret had seen me looking at this and that and was pleasantly ready to answer my questions. So I said: 'I saw a chair just like this in the V. and A. Museum the other day.' It was a very beautiful chair. Margaret nodded, and told me it was a copy, but an old copy. The chair I had seen was Elizabethan, so I sat down cautiously.

The tea table had an unusual appearance. There were two loaves of bread, one brown, one white, a dish of butter, a bowl with lettuce in it, a dish with a cucumber on it and there was a homemade cream cheese. In front of Margaret's plate was a small plate with two or three oatmeal biscuits – these were for her. I wished I had them in front of me. But Ivy had other plans for me.

'I hope you like bread and butter,' she said, as she cut the loaf. 'There is no cake. Will you have brown or white?'

Ivy put a slice of brown on my plate. Then she cut a good inch of cucumber and put that on my plate, took up a handful of lettuce, shook a quantity of water over the Persian rug, and put that on my plate.

'Take some cream cheese,' she commanded. 'There, in front of you.' All resistance gone, I did as I was told. I was kept very busy with my lettuce and cucumber and cream cheese and bread and butter, and was rather slow. Ivy, on the other hand, managed it all with brisk efficiency and obvious relish, shredding her cucumber finely, breaking up her lettuce, spreading cheese over her slice of bread, helping us to tea, keeping the conversation going and popping more cucumber or lettuce on one's plate if one didn't watch out.

Margaret took no part in these antics. She watched us with her lazy smile, crumbling her oatmeal biscuit while we ate our cucumber.

'Have some more cucumber?' Ivy said.

'No thank-you very much . . . it was delicious.'

'Ivy eats cucumbers as soon as they appear in the shops,' Margaret said.

'They have a very short season, really,' Ivy said.

I asked if she had always liked them, and Ivy said yes, always.

'And meringues,' Margaret said. 'The nice sticky kind.'

'Oh, you can't get them now,' Ivy said.

Tea at Braemar Mansions was a long drawn-out meal. It changed with the years, more drawn-out, I think never under two hours – and much less of a meal – the usual tea food, cake, toast (Ivy loved toast), but one was allowed a biscuit if one liked. I can't say just when Ivy gave up the lettuce and cheese and cucumber teas, but suddenly, to my huge relief, they were of the past. And the scene for tea shifted from the sitting-room to the dining-room.

When I look back to that time, when Ivy sliced up her cucumbers and enjoyed her lettuce and cream cheese, while Margaret looked on with her delightful, lazy smile, I am sure it was a time when Ivy was happiest.

The friendship between the two women was a deep one. It was a marriage of true minds, one that lasted for over thirty years. There is a passage in *Dolores* on such a friendship: it is a passage with the over-weightedness of immaturity.

'There was that in Dolores which yielded to womanhood's spells. She hardly judged of women as a woman amongst them; but as something sterner and stronger, that owed them gentleness in judgment. From the

35

first hour to the last of their years of friendship, she read Perdita as an open page; and loved her with a love that grew, though its nurture was not in what she read.'

(The word judgment is spelt without the e. A printer's error, or perhaps Ivy missed it when proof-reading?)

Ivy saw the mature women of her novels as 'fulfilled'. In a Platonic sense one saw Ivy and Margaret as having fulfilled themselves, their union a fruitful one, the bond between them, as Plato says in *The Symposium* 'stronger than between ordinary parents . . . the children they shared surpassing human children by being immortal . . .'

In *The Present and the Past* Miss Ridley says:' . . . producing something that exists outside yourself – that is a great thing to feel.'

Ivy and Margaret stimulated each other. And their published work, though altogether different in style and presentation and form was, nevertheless, complementary. Margaret was an expert on the furnishings and decoration and architecture of the great houses of England, the stately homes. Ivy wrote about the squirearchy of the Victorian and early Edwardian times, the landed gentry, the 'carriage folk' as they were called. These lived in the houses that Margaret described. Not quite so 'stately' as Margaret's, but 'places', with their farms and acres, their tenants and their servants.

To Ivy and Margaret I was a creature from another world: I worked for my living. When I first knew them we had a Socialist Government. I remember once during tea Ivy heard me tell Margaret that I helped a doctor with his secretarial work two or three times a week. Ivy put down her cup and looked at me severely.

'But not one of those doctors employed by the Government, I hope?'

I said no, he was not one of those. He had decided to keep his practice private.

'Have nothing to do with those other doctors,' Ivy warned. 'Poor Rose Macaulay made the dreadful mistake of going to a Government dentist,' she went on. 'Now she has broken her plate, and she has to speak at some place next week, and they tell her it won't be ready for a month.'

Ivy sometimes talked like someone out of Cranford. And Margaret had the same vagueness about ordinary, practical matters. It was typical of Rose Macaulay to put herself under the National Health Service; when she wanted to give her young god-children a holiday she took them off to Butlin's Holiday Camp for a week. I don't know if she ever told Ivy and Margaret about it: they would not have understood about Butlin's.

We often talked about our holidays and our trips abroad. When a book was finished and in the hands of their publishers, they felt they had earned a holiday. At this time, just after the war, when Ivy had finished *Manservant and Maidservant*, travel abroad was both difficult and expensive. Ivy and Margaret decided to go to St Cast in Brittany.

'We couldn't have gone if we hadn't each finished a book,' Ivy said later, when they came back.

'And we stayed in a convent,' Margaret said. 'If you don't insist on having wine with all your meals, a convent is the best place.'

In spite of the cucumbers I enjoyed these teas. Conversation was easy with Margaret there. She was a fluent and ready talker, I was no talker at all, but I asked questions about Hepplewhite and Japanese mirror painting and Knowle, and Ivy listened to Margaret, proud and respectful.

Once, the subject of friends sharing a flat came up. My sister and I had shared a flat, or rather a maisonnette, I think it was called, with two friends. It meant, I told them, that we each had a bed-sitting-room, a good arrangement. Margaret asked if we could not share a sitting-room. I said yes, my sister and I could quite happily. But our two friends were separate. We had our meals together, then we went our separate ways. Margaret told me that several of her friends shared a home, but insisted on separate sitting-rooms. I said, yes, of course. But Margaret thought this extraordinary, that *friends*, two friends, were unable to share a sitting-room.

During the war the two friends had stayed with a friend in Cambridgeshire. Ivy told me they had returned once or twice to their flat in Linden Gardens. The neighbourhood of Notting Hill Gate had suffered rather badly in the Blitz, and I mentioned this to Ivy. I had been on duty at a first-aid post there and I remembered our casualties.

Ivy agreed. She said: 'I wanted to see how Margaret would stand the bombing.'

I thought the remark a strange one at the time, but now, looking back, it seems quite characteristic of Ivy. Disciplined herself, she expected discipline of her friend.

And from my first meetings with her I gradually saw her as a woman with a nature and temperament altogether more masculine than feminine. She was always gentle and quiet in manner, but she seemed as well to have such steely weapons mentally that I often thought of the old saying about the mailed fist in the velvet glove. Certainly there was nothing in the least feminine or 'cosy' about the flat. The sitting-room was austere, and so was her bedroom. Her bathroom and lavatory were never modernised during the thirty odd years she lived in Braemar Mansions. Years after we had all given our baths that 'built-in' look, Ivy's bath kept its legs sticking out like museum pieces. And the lavatory kept its clanking old chain when everyone else had what house-agents call 'low flush toilets'. Yet Ivy and Margaret had more or less wrecked a wall in each of two flats in order to save an Adam mantelpiece. My sense of values was inferior: I would have chosen a modern bathroom and let the mantelpiece go. I sometimes felt like a creature from another planet, and for years I had this feeling of separateness from Ivy – but not from Margaret –

I always did as I was told and ate up my cucumber like a good girl, but Margaret also could be sharply corrected for any breach of decorum. I remember on one very hot afternoon when we were at the tea table, Margaret, who had been out, drank her tea thirstily and passed her cup up to Ivy to be re-filled. Not a word was said, but Ivy's displeasure sent the temperature to below zero. She took Margaret's cup in stern silence, put it down, and held out her hand for my cup, which, unfortunately for Margaret, was empty. I kept my expression blank, but stole a glance at Margaret who was watching the pantomime with smiling indulgence.

'I was very thirsty,' she said. 'It's really very hot today.'

Ivy's severities with such peccadilloes was both amusing and surprising to a third person, especially to one who knew her books well. It seemed to me one might expect a little tolerance from an author with such a relish for crime. But Ivy was never too prim for crime, it was simply she insisted on good manners. Her villains are all as elegantly civilised as Browning's Duke in *My Last Duchess*. This insistence on good manners runs like a thread through her written work.

> 'Nothing goes deeper than manners . . . they are involved with the whole of life. It is they that give rise to it, and come to depend on it. We should all remember it.'

This is from her last, unfinished novel *The Last and the First*.

Reading that now, with sadness, it is some comfort that in all the years one knew her one would never dream of contradicting her, and it cost nothing to take a reproof, when it came, meekly. And of course her reproofs did not come often. When she was sharp, one remembered it. And even her sharpness was worth having. Ivy often used the phrase 'barely uttered' in her books, when one of her characters makes some remark with an especial edge to it, something the butler, perhaps, flings over his shoulder as he leaves the dining-room, 'barely uttering' the barbed remark.

Ivy once 'barely uttered' at me. It was not long after Margaret's death, and she was still in a state of strain. We were at lunch, and were having dessert. Ivy was eating a date or two, and I was eating walnuts. Dates are sticky things, and Ivy looked at me and said: 'You have your finger bowl.'

I glanced at it, thinking I hardly needed it after a couple of walnuts, but that I had better use it since there it was.

'Wake up!'

This was 'barely uttered', a sort of sighing whisper which I pretended not to hear. I had only delayed movement by about half-a-minute, but the half-minute had been too long for Ivy.

I used my finger bowl and remarked on its beauty.

2

Before *Manservant and Maidservant* was published I had been to Hanover with the Control Commission of Germany to see what could be done with a bilingual magazine or journal aimed at university students and young poets and writers. We found a suitable German editor, a young man called Rudolf Jung, and our scheme went apace and the journal ran for three years. A huge success with the bewildered and defeated Germans, but unfortunately they could not pay for their copies. In England our support came from German scholars, a society called the Goethe Society, refugee German Jews and pacifists. English contributors wrote on Goethe and Rilke and Thomas Mann and the Germans wrote on Virginia Woolf and T. S. Eliot and Aldous Huxley. No one wrote on Ivy Compton-Burnett, but Rudolf Jung knew of my admiration for her and asked if she had ever been translated into German. He knew, he told me, Hans Wagenseil who was brilliant at translation work and was Virginia Woolf's translator. Ivy liked the idea of having him to translate *A House and its Head* and asked me to bring Rudolf to tea. He remembers nothing of the tea-party except his awe of Ivy and the charm of Margaret Jourdain. I remember his speaking of his admiration for Charles Morgan which provoked a groan of disapproval from me, and a quick look at Ivy as I didn't know what her feelings about him were. Ivy said smoothly, and quietly: 'I think him awful. Have some more lettuce,' while Rudolf went on talking about Morgan to Margaret who listened with her usual courtesy.

Later I sent my precious copy of *A House and Its Head* – the first edition from Boot's Library – to Hans Wagenseil who found the book 'extremely difficult', and quite the hardest he had ever been asked to translate.

Manservant and Maidservant was published early in 1947, and Ivy wrote to me in March of that year.

5, Braemar Mansions,
Cornwall Gardens. S.W.7.
March 1947

Dear Miss Greig,

I am glad indeed to hear that A House and its Head is to go into German, and to be so well translated.

I quite agree that the notices of my new book are lacking in judgment and insight. So far I think the New Statesman is the best.

Curtis Brown is indeed sadly in need of the goad. They are so short-handed that there seems to be no help for it.

It will be best for you to write to the Control Commission yourself, and when it comes to Curtis Brown tell them that you have my sanction, and I will confirm what you say.

I greatly appreciate your interest and kindness. You will let me know if there is any expense involved.

Yours sincerely,
Ivy Compton-Burnett.

The odd thing about this letter is that Ivy spells judgment without the e. It was the way I spelt the word, and she may have had my letter in front of her, not a very likely explanation.

The word *goad* is typical. She was fastidious in her choice of a word; it had to convey her meaning as exactly as possible. We might say that So-and-So wanted shaking up – one of our loose modern phrases. Ivy felt that her agents wanted to be spurred on to more decisive action. She was always reluctant to use the word or phrase that lay to her hand, the ready-made one. In *Manservant and Maidservant*, for instance, when Gideon returns home from his tutoring, his sister Magdalen brings him 'a restorative'. I suppose that was a drink, but Ivy would never have used the word as we do, on its own. She criticised the unusual words that novelists used. We spoke of this habit once, and I said that poets like to use unusual words, and I thought it not a bad thing for novelists to do the same.

'But they use words that aren't in the dictionary,' she declared. 'I've looked them up and they aren't there.'

On the other hand she used words that have almost passed out of normal speech. In *Brothers and Sisters*, for instance, she describes a house, and then the garden:

'It did not do even as well' – (as the house) – unless the purpose of a garden is to accommodate a moderate quantity of potsherds, and a considerable one of properties the neighbourhood finds dispensable.'

This Victorian way of saying the garden had become a rubbish dump is quite one of Ivy's worst sentences, and worthy of Professor Saintsbury. But *Brothers and Sisters* is an early book – it was published in 1929, and Ivy had not quite found her famous rhythm. The word potsherds is archaic today. Perhaps it was still in use in 1929.

Sometimes these unusual words came out in her conversation, really not surprising when one considers that all her novels are of Victorian or Edwardian times. I remember at lunch once the maid brought in the pudding and put it in front of Ivy. It was a kind of *mousse*, and it had been . . .

'When I was young,' Ivy told me, as soon as the door was closed, 'it was considered to be a breach of etiquette to bring a dish to the table that had been broached.'

In this letter Ivy mentions that the reviews of *Manservant and Maidservant* were lacking in judgment and insight. This was always the case, and her reviews were always mixed. Some critics were enthusiastic, others found her altogether too difficult, and said her plots had no relation to the happenings of normal life, which was unfair. *The Times Literary Supplement* gave their middle page to their review of the book and the *New Statesman* usually reviewed her as she liked to be reviewed. In later years critics looked back to this novel as her 'masterpiece'. But by far the best reviews, in my opinion, appeared in the leading American literary journals. The title, *Manservant and Maidservant* was rejected by the American publisher, and the novel appeared under the title of *Bullivant and the Lambs*, rather a good title, I thought. I always disliked the word maidservant though I would never dare tell Ivy of this peculiarity of mine. I happened to see two or three of the American journals and took them with me to Braemar Mansions when I had to call for some of Margaret's work. Ivy had asked me to call just after lunch, and I had coffee with them. I produced the papers, and told Ivy I thought the critics over there were wittier and more intelligent about her work and altogether more enthusiastic than the English critics. Ivy put the journals on one side and with her quiet courtesy listened to what I was saying, and she and I discussed the business of reviewing and being reviewed while we drank our coffee. But Margaret snatched up the copy of *Time* I had brought, when I told them I thought the review in that was the best of all, and while Ivy and I talked Margaret read it with close attention. My chair was facing her and I was able to watch her as she read it. I remember her expression when she had finished reading it, *Time* still in her hands, but her eyes on Ivy's face, her expression glowing with pride. We talked on, Ivy and I, but Margaret was silent, looking at Ivy with a sort of wonder. In a moment, of course, Ivy caught her look, understood it, and turned back to me.

'Do have another cup of coffee,' she said.

Margaret had not said a word, but there was an urgency in her look that fairly drove me away. I made some excuse about another appointment, and stood up to go. Ivy insisted on seeing me to the front door.

'I don't of course want those papers back,' I said. 'A friend lets me have them.'

Ivy said she would enjoy reading them, thanked me, and I left. I tried to imagine the scene between the two friends.

I think this novel of Ivy's was the one to establish her firmly as an important novelist of our time. Certainly more interest was shown in her and her work from this time, more authors wrote to her, and students, saying they had chosen her work as a subject for their theses. A neighbour of mine who had written many non-fiction books told me she had written to Ivy to invite her to lunch, and Ivy had accepted. She asked me what Ivy was like. I said 'She's unique in every way,' and left it at that. They met over the lunch table, and we met again, being near neighbours.

'Well, you met Ivy Compton-Burnett?'

Yes, Ivy had come to lunch.

'Very interesting meeting her,' my neighbour said. 'But she's cagey. Don't you find she's cagey?'

But Ivy was not cagey. One crossed whole areas of silence when one talked with her, but that quiet of hers was not so much a barricade as an interest in one. There was a wariness in her silent attention, but I am sure it had a creative quality, she was a keen observer of human behaviour.

It was after the publication of *Manservant and Maidservant* that Cecil Beaton decided to photograph her. Ivy told me about the experience one day during tea.

'He was more interested in the furniture, I think,' she said. 'He asked me to sit on that chair – ' She pointed to a chair that stood between the two small firescreens. 'I told him it was broken, and might give way. He just said: "Yes, but you will sit on it for *me*, won't you?" '

Another photograph of her was taken with her back to her long French windows, so that the opposite house formed a background.

The caption read: 'Ivy Compton-Burnett ought not to be outlined in profile against a South Kensington house-front. Her permanent situation – to judge from her books – is squarely in front of an overgrown vicarage full of children and aunts and grandparents.'

Her houses, the setting of her novels, are not vicarages.

Photographs always made her look older, and Cecil Beaton made her look sinister, perhaps thinking of her tyrants.

There have been many photographs of her, but I have never seen one I liked; none of them were quite Ivy, and many were not her at all. Photographers like line and bone structure, and wanting this they made her tilt her head upwards, some of them, so that her chin appeared to jut menacingly. She had a strong face, but her chin was not at all the jutting kind, and there was no hardness in the lines of her mouth. Each feature of her face bore the distinct mark of an inward trait. Her small, arched nose was not arrogant but it suggested the classic austerity of her thought. Her mouth, on the other hand, showed a great sweetness and gentleness of character. Her humour was in her eyes, wonderfully expressive green-grey eyes. I never heard her laugh, but I have often seen laughter in her eyes. At other times they were watchful, wary, sometimes hostile. She was an ivory tower, and one had to climb her stair. Once or twice I tried to bring her out of her tower, but her look dared me to venture too far.

When I typed her novels and came to those precise feature by feature descriptions of each character, I sometimes tried to relate them to those friends of hers I had met at Braemar Mansions. But I have only twice thought that I recognised a clear portrait. One was in the description of Maria Shelley in *Two Worlds and their Ways* which I typed in 1948. Maria Shelley was 53, with a broad massive frame and a crumpled, weather-beaten face. Of course Margaret Jourdain was not like that, but when I typed those words they at once suggested her to me. And in Ivy's last novel her description of Jocasta, a grandmother of eighty-four – Ivy's age when she was writing the book – with her 'alert look' suggested Ivy to me at once. Jocasta, however, is a tall old lady and Ivy was very small. There was never any doubt in my mind that Mortimer of *Manservant and Maidservant* was a distant portrait of Ernest Thesiger. This distinguished actor lived near Ivy, and his wife Janet had shared a flat with Margaret Jourdain before she married Ernest.

Ivy always said that once she had finished a novel she felt drained, and she even used the stock phrase – not a habit of hers – that virtue had gone out of her. But in spite of this, and of her saying she could not consider herself as a professional writer, her output was regular from 1929, when *Brothers and Sisters* was published, to 1963 when *A God and his Gifts* came out. I typed *Manservant and Maidservant* in March 1946 and it came out in February 1947. By the summer of the following year Ivy had another manuscript ready for me, *Two Worlds and their Ways*. This was published in June 1949. This pattern of work was fairly regular during these years up to 1963, and is really a remarkable achievement when one remembers that she was never a young writer.

For my own interest I set out the publication dates of all her novels from 1911, when *Dolores* was published, and her age at the time. I include *Dolores* because of the time-gap between its publication and that of *Pastors and Masters* (1925).

Ivy's birthday was in June, and I have not checked her age with the exact date of the publication of each novel, only going by the year.

1911	*Dolores*	age 27
1925	*Pastors and Masters*	41
1929	*Brothers and Sisters*	45
1931	*Men and Wives*	47
1933	*More Women than Men*	49
1935	*A House and Its Head*	51
1937	*Daughters and Sons*	53
1939	*A Family and a Fortune*	55
1941	*Parents and Children*	57
1944	*Elders and Betters*	59
1947	*Manservant and Maidservant*	63
1949	*Two Worlds and their Ways*	65
1951	*Darkness and Day*	67
1953	*The Present and the Past*	69
1955	*Mother and Son*	71
1957	*A Father and his Fate*	73
1959	*A Heritage and its History*	75
1961	*The Mighty and their Fall*	77
1963	*A God and his Gifts*	79
1969	*The Last and The First*	85

When I went to Braemar Mansions to fetch the Manuscript of *Two Worlds and their Ways* the two friends had just returned from a short holiday in a remote part of Buckinghamshire.

'Did you know?' Ivy asked me, 'that there are still some cottages in England without water?'

Of course I knew, everybody knew, but I could hardly say so. Ivy knew nothing about the normal day-to-day living conditions of the working class, and very little about ordinary everyday life. There was nothing ordinary about Ivy, about her books, about the characters she created. Neither she nor Margaret could be called ordinary. But Margaret was the daughter of a country vicar and should have had some awareness of the slow rate of progress in remote villages. But it seems she had forgotten. She said: 'It was a hot day, and we had walked rather far, and I was thirsty. So we knocked on the door of a cottage and I asked if I could have a drink of water. They told us they had no water in the house. No taps and no drains. They shared a pump with other cottages.'

They reminded me of those two women, Eleanor Jourdain and Annie Moberley, who wandered about Versailles and met with the strange ghosts of old, unhappy, far-off days. David Garnett confused Eleanor with Margaret in his autobiography, which annoyed Ivy. I have a note from her dated 5 December 1955 mentioning this:

'David Garnett confused Eleanor Jourdain and Miss Moberley with Margaret Jourdain and me, and has caused quite a lot of question and explanation, but people seem to understand. His book has many blunders.'

The book was *The Flowers of the Forest*, the second volume of David Garnett's memoirs, published in 1955. The author refers to Frankie Birrell's habit of falling asleep when tired or bored, and to one particular evening, a year or two after the Armistice of 1918.

He had gone to dinner with two elderly spinsters, one being Miss Margaret Jourdain and the other, I believe, Miss C. A. E. Moberly, who had achieved fame by writing, in collaboration, *An Adventure*, an account of falling into the eighteenth century during perambulations of *Le Petit Trianon*, apparently by a mixture of time-travelling and telepathy. The ladies maintained that their story was true and carried out considerable historical researches to prove its accuracy.

Miss Jourdain was also an authority on old furniture and wrote articles on it for *The Burlington Magazine* and *Country Life*. She had many choice pieces in her collection. Both were cultured, intelligent women who enjoyed Frankie's conversation, but they were not intimate friends.

'I can quite clearly remember the soup,' said Frankie, wrinkling his brows. 'Then, I suppose, we must have had fish, because when I woke up

46

there *was* a plate of fish, uneaten, in front of me. As a matter of fact my left hand was in it, covered with sauce. I was alone in the dining-room; the lights were burning, and when I looked at my watch I saw that it was past midnight. The ladies seemed to have gone to bed.'

David Garnett corrected what he calls his 'deplorable mistake' in an errata list in his third volume *Familiar Faces*, published in 1962. His Errata note reads:

The Golden Echo p. 209 from line 7
the passage should read: had gone to dinner with two ladies, Miss Margaret Jourdain and Miss Ivy Compton-Burnett. Miss Jourdain had written many books on old furniture and wrote regularly on it for *Country Life*. Her young friend Miss Compton-Burnett, had not at that time published any books and her literary genius was altogether unsuspected. It was, if not Frankie's first visit to their house, the first time he had been asked to dinner. The ladies had been charmed by him at first meeting, but they were not intimate friends of his.

Ivy had published *Dolores*, but that was probably unknown. The dinner must have taken place in the early twenties and before *Pastors and Masters* was published. Eleanor Jourdain was Margaret's sister, and of course it is known now that what she and Miss Moberley saw that day as they wandered about *Le Petit Trianon* was no trick of the imagination. The people were real, guests at a fancy dress party.

David Garnett relates that 'the ladies' forgave Frankie, he received another invitation, the friendship 'cemented by the disasters of that evening'. The chief disaster was that Frankie asleep had leaned too heavily on the arm of his chair and it was broken when he woke up. The chair was Louis Quinze.

Frankie Birrell died about ten years later, January 1935, of tumour of the brain.

I bore away the manuscript of *Two Worlds and their Ways* and began to type it at once. One remark in the first paragraph of the opening breakfast scene was authentic Ivy 'at home', and I had heard the remark, or something like it, more than once.

'The money subscribed divided by the number of subscribers gives you the average subscription. Twenty-four pounds ten shillings and sixpence, divided by thirty-five. Would you do a sum like that in your head, Roderick? Or could you not do it at all?'

The last question 'Or could you not do it at all', with Ivy took the form of 'or don't you know?'

'People tell me I should cut down my fuchsias now,' she told me in the spring. 'Just when they are making fresh growth. Ought we to do that, just at this time? Or don't you know?'

Given my cue I said at once that I didn't know. Since then I have learnt that one should cut them down otherwise they go to leaf. Another time the question was on chickens, whether the chickens one bought in London stores – that were so tasteless – came from the same farms as those one enjoyed so much in country homes – 'or don't you know'? 'Why is everything frozen nowadays?' she asked me, years later (when everything was frozen) – 'Why are there so many black faces in London nowadays?' 'Or don't you know?' I used to wait for it, though it was said in the same breath as the question, pushing my hand against my mouth to smother my smile.

When I read *Two Worlds and their Ways* later, I found that those chapters describing how the two children were under some over-mastering compulsion to cheat in order that they might succeed, distressed me. They were tragic figures, and I thought Ivy had pushed her imagination too far. This of course is unfair criticism. One must accept whatever a classical writer sees as possible. I had learned not to question Ivy's plots long before I met her. She had an Elizabethan's relish for dark intrigue. Others abide our question, like Shakespeare, like Sophocles, she is free.

But typing the book was a delight. It is full of humour, of fun, of witty talk. Eleven year old schoolboys discuss concubines.

'Do all men who can afford to, keep concubines?'

'No, only in China. In England only a few keep them. And they are generally kept outside the house. Sometimes the real wife does not know about them.'

'I am the son of a real wife,' said Sefton, with tears in his voice. 'My father's first wife died before he ever saw my mother.'

'Well, there is no need to cry about it,' said Bacon. 'Your father may love your mother the best. That does happen with concubines. I daresay Agamemnon loved Cassandra better than Clytaemnestra. Indeed it seems as if he did.'

'How do you know so much about concubines? Do all your fathers keep several?'

The talk between the male adults, especially the young schoolmasters and Juliet Cassidy, one of Ivy's witty and intelligent women, a type that occurs in more than one novel – is especially good. There is the character too, also in other novels, unable to keep pace with the others, and the talk is slowed down by her protests. Maria Shelley says, in some bewilderment at the cracking pace of the talk: 'Is this talk supposed to be clever?' Her stepson answers: 'Well, yes, Maria, it is . . .' Maria complains: 'I am so wearied by this quibbling with words that mean nothing, when there is a real problem hanging over us. . . . I hope you like to hear me speaking like a woman,' Maria goes on, 'because I am going to do so. Could we manage without a subject and just talk of anything that comes into our heads?'

'Well, honestly, Maria, that is what we have been doing,' Lesbia tells her.

The sophisticated win in the end. They have the weapons. But Juliet is to say, later: '. . . cynicism has no place in life, though it will make conversation very difficult. No one will be able to be clever.'

I always enjoyed taking the finished typescript, both top and carbon copies bound as neatly as I could manage – though I was never very expert at this – to Braemar Mansions. Ivy never opened the parcel to look at it. She put it on her desk and after asking me how I fared, and offering me coffee, or tea, or sherry, according to the time of day, she would take out her cheque book and insist on settling the account at once.

'Don't bother with a receipt. I don't want one,' she always said.

And I always answered: 'Oh, you must have one. For your Income tax returns. I'm one of your necessary expenses.'

This was a period when we were on the most formal terms. It was many years before we reached the stage of calling each other by our Christian names and kissing each other on meeting. In those early years I thought Ivy would never unbend, and not being unbent to, I decided it would be necessary for me to play this formal game with her, rather like learning the steps of a quadrille. Ivy was such a period piece – late Victorian and early Edwardian – that she could only see me as a creature of that time. I was educated, yes, 'but obliged to earn her living, poor thing'. I was of the governess class, I decided. Once I had solved this little problem of our relationship I was quite happy and content 'to keep my place'. Ivy's children were her novels, and they were put into my charge . . . it was a game I could play with her. I enjoyed my part, and our relationship was always a smooth one. I sometimes envied the bounce her governesses had – her Miss Hallam or her Miss Starkie, for instance, irrepressible and quite unsnubbable.

I should like to have come in, one cloudy day, with my improving little message.

'Now, Miss Compton-Burnett, we shall have to have sunshine in ourselves today. There is none outside for us. But that should not be difficult for fortunate people like ourselves.'

Two Worlds and their Ways came out in June 1949, her birthday month. She was sixty-five. Most of the reviews of the book appeared in the same month. When I read *Two Worlds and their Ways* I thought it quite a gripping story, and on the whole quite amusing. But most of the reviewers wrote of the 'intense concentration' Ivy demanded of her readers. C. P. Snow wrote:

> 'In order to read this novelist at all, much more to get the maximum out of her work, the reader has to perform a creative act himself; he has to supply the glue which sticks novels together, the ordinary commonplaces which make them real in terms of human sense. No novelist has ever asked so much from her readers; I think it is too much.'

This criticism from a writer like C. P. Snow amazed us.

The novel seems to have frightened Elizabeth Jenkins quite out of her wits. I never quite knew what the phrase meant until I read her review.

> 'The work is frightening because it is in the true descent of English fiction – and this is what the family has come to. This dehydrated form of imaginative writing is one aspect of the Zeitgeist, of which artificial insemination and the atomic bomb are another.'

Poor Ivy. And how we laughed over that one!

But Philip Toynbee, reviewing the novel in the *New Statesman* seems to complain that Ivy's novels are not frightening enough. Her plots, he says,

> 'do not harrow us or purge us, and we live in a sad age when not to be harrowed is not to be wholly won. We can only give full admiration where we have ourselves been given pain. Nor is this demand so perverted as it might seem in this bare form. In so far as she fails to disturb us, Miss Compton-Burnett fails.'

I don't think reviews like that disturbed Ivy, or gave her pain, and I am quite certain she thought, as reviews, they had failed. She subscribed to a press-cutting agency, and showed especial interest in what other novelists wrote of her. She always said she was grateful for a good criticism. She tried to make resolutions based on these criticisms, as she often told interviewers, but this was not easy for her. She was aware that her circle of readers, here and in the United States, was a small one, but it was enthusiastic and loyal. She would never be a popular writer, but once discovered, her unquestionable gifts won her love and homage and loyalty from an ever widening circle of friends. A classic writer can never be a craze. She escaped the peril of popularity. And other perils could do her no harm. Because, of course, the very fact that she was extraordinary pushed some to the conclusion that she was more extraordinary than she really was, like the cartoonists who drew her, in her last year or two, almost witchlike. Madame Sarraute hailed her as 'one of our greatest novelists' because, herself a great one for experiment, she saw in Ivy's dialogue those *tropisms* or sub-conversations that 'no inner language can convey'. She made her pilgrimage from Paris to Braemar Mansions some time after the war, and I got the impression that Ivy was not quite certain what Madame Sarraute was about. I should like to have been present at this meeting between a prominent and distinguished French intellectual of the Sartre or post-Sartre period, and an English intellectual of the Victorian-Edwardian period. It was a mission of homage to Ivy on Madame Sarraute's part, and Ivy of course accepted the compliment with her usual modesty and courteous hospitality, asking Madame Sarraute if French cakes were as good as ever, and telling her that in England cakes one bought were not as good as those one bought before the war.

I am not a French scholar but critics have called Madame Sarraute a disciple of Ivy Compton-Burnett – notably Bernard McCabe and Christine Brooke-Rose. And there is a passage in Madame Sarraute's novel *The Golden Fruits* – a translation by Maria Jolas – that points directly to Ivy. The book is about a book, the writing of which is so outstanding and original that critics are bewildered and hardly know whether to praise it or condemn it. But one reviewer writes this paragraph on the book's style:

'No critic will ever praise enough, ever prescribe with enough severity this written language that sifts, refines, purifies, compresses between its firm somewhat rigid contours, arranges, constructs, hardens what should endure.'

When I read that I was certain it was Nathalie Sarraute's tribute to Ivy's style.

About this time, two or three of us were working on an anthology which we called *The Adventurers*. We wanted to trace the history of adventurous writing in prose and poetry in English literature. It was to start with the Elizabethans, Spenser and Sidney and Lyly and Stanyhurst and on through the centuries to Doughty, who wrote Spenserian English, and to our contemporaries. There were many adventurers and I found the research absorbing. Michael Hamburger looked after the section dealing with modern poetry. It was while I was working on women novelists – Dorothy Richardson, Virginia Woolf and Elizabeth Bowen, that I decided to ask Ivy if I could include her. First I wrote a short piece on her way of writing, really a précis of what I wanted to say, with quotations from her novels.

When next I was asked to tea I told Ivy what we were doing, and I told her we would like to include her if she was agreeable. I said I had written a paragraph giving the gist of what I wanted to say. Of course I had plenty of work still to do.

Margaret said: 'I can't see that Ivy has experimented in any way, I mean in her actual writing.'

I said that nevertheless she was such an original I thought she should be included.

'Well, let's hear what you've written,' Ivy said.

I had meant to leave my piece with her to read, not recite it like a schoolgirl.

'Oh, I thought perhaps if I left it with you you could read it some time. There's no particular hurry, of course,' I said.

But Ivy said she would like me to read it, and both she and Margaret settled themselves in their chairs, and looked at me attentively.

I read my piece about her, and perhaps I had better quote it as the reactions of Ivy and Margaret were interesting. I said that one of her innovations was balance:

> . . . action and re-action, climax and anti-climax, a general questioning and answering, so perfect that there is nothing like it in the history of the novel in England, and one must go back to the strophe and anti-strophe of a Greek chorus for comparison. This balance makes for a wonderful archi-techtonic effect; not only that, but within the complex and skilful design, observations on human behaviour, on human relationships, on the whole business of living and letting others live, hold a profounder truth, clear, brave and devoid of sentiment. Her presentation of life is so logical that when we have finished a novel by her we almost expect to find the letters Q.E.D. after the last full-stop.

Well, that was what I thought in 1949, and it all sounds a bit pompous now. And I remember reading it out to them with a beating heart.

As Ivy would say: 'There was a pause.'

Then Margaret said: 'Yes. That's very good. And it's all quite true. But it still doesn't make her an experimental writer, in my opinion. I mean, is her actual *writing* experimental?'

Before I could answer Ivy said: 'But I *want* that to be said of me. I like it very much. I should like to be included in this book.'

She spoke half-humorously, but she meant what she said. And from that moment she helped me in every way she could, telling me to come to tea on a certain day.

'Miss Jourdain has to go North next week. A museum wants her to advise them on the purchase of an antique. She's written to tell them that her fee will be fifty guineas, and they still want her to advise them.'

Ivy, on that afternoon when we were alone together, was full of encouragement, wise, gentle, wonderfully courteous in the way she listened to my ideas about the anthology. She offered me any book of hers, and took me into the dining-room, a room I had not seen before. This was a dark room, the window looking on to the well of the house, but a beautiful Welsh dresser holding rare china and some lovely blue glass made it immediately interesting when one opened the door. There were Hepplewhite chairs with her tapestry-worked seats, and a sideboard that always held several bowls of fruit, which Ivy loved. Against the wall on the right of the door was a wide cupboard that almost reached the ceiling.

'We had that cupboard made out of some shutters,' Ivy told me.

The shutters were painted white, and the cupboard held all their unsold books. Ivy offered me any of hers that I might like. I said no, if I want one that perhaps I haven't got – and I had most of her books – I would buy it. I felt we ought to buy an author's books, not get them for nothing. But they were all first editions and it wasn't very clever of me to refuse her offer, and I have regretted this always.

Before I left Ivy told me that she was getting on with another novel and I said I was all the more grateful to her for having given me so much of her time.

'I hope I can get a book published one day,' I said.

'Oh, but you obviously will,' Ivy said, to encourage me.

About this time I finished typing a book on William Kent that Margaret Jourdain had been writing. Now she turned to articles for *Country Life*, an article on Japanese Mirror Painting, and articles on the treasures of Knowle. Sometimes there was an interval of two or three months when neither Ivy nor Margaret wanted me, and during one of these spells, in the spring and early summer of 1950, troubles beset me. My father died in March – he and Ivy were attended by the same doctor in Kensington. Then in April I suddenly fell ill and had to go to hospital for three weeks. My doctor, Annis Gillie, now retired, was an ardent admirer of Ivy's novels. I went to Sussex for my convalescence and made up my mind to find some flat or cottage where I could live and work quietly in the country. In my rather frail state London seemed really terrifying – noisy, hurried and violent. I returned to London, and cousins in Sussex promised to look out for some suitable accommodation for me. On 2 July there was a postcard from Ivy.

'Can you type a novel for me? Not very long this time. I hope you are not too busy.'

This was good news, and I went off to collect the manuscript the next morning. Both Ivy and Margaret were in the sitting-room, and when I told them I had been ill we all had a glass of sherry, and they drank to my good health.

When Ivy had just finished a novel there were usually signs of strain, and on this occasion these signs were more marked than usual. Margaret talked to me, telling me they were going away – 'now that we've each got a book done' – but Ivy, apart from her first greeting and enquiries, remained withdrawn. Now and then a slight whispering sound escaped her, as though she was talking to herself. I wondered if she was repeating some snatch of conversation from her book. She certainly took no part in the short exchange Margaret and I had together over a quick glass of sherry. I noticed too that when Ivy stood up when I said goodbye, she limped, and I had to hold on to her.

'I have a sore foot,' she told me. 'So I won't go to the door with you.'

In spite of my protests that of course I would see myself out, Margaret walked with me to the front door. She said goodbye, and hoped I would soon be quite well. I told her I really felt much better, and I added that I hoped Ivy would feel better after a holiday.

'I thought she seemed not very well,' I said.

To my surprise Margaret looked at me with a sort of anguish, and cried: 'She's *very well*,' with bitter emphasis on each word.

She turned and rushed back to the sitting-room.

It was the last time I saw her. She died the following April. I had intruded clumsily into that earthly paradise of perfect friendship, and thought of this later with grief.

As soon as I reached my flat I opened the parcel Ivy had given me. There were the usual exercise books, and one of Ivy's little notes to me clipped to the cover of the first one. This was the last of these little notes. Perhaps after three novels she had decided I no longer needed reminding of what I must and must not do. Here is her note, written in pencil, like her novel.

Please do it all yourself.
   „   do not omit any punctuation, as it is all intended.
// = new paragraph.
Please do not take books to pieces. But you never do.
Please put fasteners so that the MS. opens flat.
1 Carbon Copy.
No great hurry. Should just like it got on with.

The title of the book was *Darkness and Day*, one of Ivy's strangest novels, one that I found depressing in parts, but with passages in it of marvellous prose-poetry.

Typing Ivy's novels was really a wonderful experience. The sentences unfold, word by word, phrase by phrase, and the different tones of the different characters are heard so much more clearly, one *reads* more with the story in mind. And here the plot is Sophoclean. Even the children, Rose and Viola, aged ten and eight, know about Oedipus. Gaunt son of Selina, and brother of Edmund, learns that his brother believes, mistakenly, that he has married his own daughter. He sums up the situation:

'Edmund has married his daughter. His children are his grandchildren. Bridget is their mother and their sister.'

Rose, aged ten, discusses this in the nursery with the nursemaid, Fanshawe.

'Of course your mamma did not do what Oedipus did,' (Fanshawe says.)
'She did it the other way round,' said Rose.
'She killed her mother instead of her father, and then married her father

55

instead of her mother. Of course she could only marry a man. And she minded as much as Oedipus, or almost as much.'

The two children are almost as horrific as the pair in James's *The Turn of the Screw*. They enjoy the company of the servants, and love Mrs Spruce – their maternal grandmother, 'as it transpires', but Mrs. Spruce would rather die than reveal it, and only Selina, their other grandmother, discovers the truth. Ambrose the Butler quotes Shakespeare, Milton and Wordsworth, and, like Bullivant, has to keep an untrained young footman, Bartle, who is seventeen, in his place. These young servants in Ivy's novels are the socialists of the future, rebels against the staunch loyalties of the elders. Mildred Hallam is one of Ivy's typically exuberant governesses, but the children defeat her, and she retreats gracefully. She has her personal triumph when it is revealed that Edmund is really her father, and the children her half-sisters. Like Mrs Spruce, she decides to keep her place, though the secret is known. It is a novel of mixed-up relationships, with no action other than the unravelling of this tangled web. The most attractive character in the novel is Sir Ransome Chace, while his friend Gaunt Lovat, with a curiosity as insatiable as that of Kipling's elephant, is one of the sharpest drawn of the characters in the book. Tragedy calls for a heightened style, and Ivy can lift hers to poetry, alliteration and all.

Edmund says to his wife:

'Yes, that is the sadness in our sorrow, that it takes the guise of shame. That is what I would spare you, if you would be spared. Shame is no less, that it is helpless, and pity may carry much that destroys itself. And we shall face it in its hardest form, the form that carries self-pity. We shall have to give pity ourselves.

Ivy was still away by the time I had finished typing *Darkness and Day*. I left the parcel of typescript and manuscript with her housekeeper and went off to Sussex for another holiday. Later I received her letter thanking me.

5, Braemar Mansions
Cornwall Gardens, S.W.7.
August 16. 1950

Dear Miss Greig,

Thank you for the typed copies of Darkness and Day. They are very nice and I am glad that the book is longer than I thought, as it is better without additions.

I am so glad that Curtis Brown are encouraging about the anthology, and I like the idea of more text myself, as the thread of things will be clearer. I shall like to talk about it very much, if you will suggest a day in September perhaps late in the month, as we may be away in the first half.

I am enclosing a cheque for the account.

Yours very sincerely,
Ivy Compton-Burnett.

I hope you will have good weather and a real rest. Don't waste stamps on the receipt.

Spencer Curtis Brown had liked the anthology as far as we had gone, and was encouraging. But he preferred more text, and that the book should be about adventurers, rather than a brief note about them and examples from their works. This was more exciting to do, and it gave one more scope, and I was glad that Ivy approved. Before I saw her in September I had heard from a cousin in Sussex that she had found a studio-flat for me in a village I knew very well. It would be vacant in November and I arranged to move down that month as soon as it was free.

Ivy strongly disapproved, and she never quite forgave me for making up my mind to leave London. The country for her was for holidays. One *lived* in London. London, she always said, 'had more to offer'. 'And in these days,' she added, 'if one stays with friends in the country one can only go where one can be certain of service.' When country walks are mentioned in *Dolores* someone, of Ivy's turn of mind, promptly quotes Dr Johnson: 'Sir, when you have seen one green field, you have seen all green fields. Sir, I like to look upon men. Let us walk down Cheapside.'

Ivy couldn't believe I would settle permanently in the country. I reminded her that there were trains. She had only to send me a post-card and I would be up at once.

In November of that year (1950) I took myself and my typewriter to my studio-flat. It belonged to a pianist whose own studio adjoined mine, both set in one large garden. Mine was partly furnished, a precaution owners always took at that time. The studio was one large, high room with a little staircase at one end leading up to a small bed-room which hung over the studio like a minstrel's gallery. There was a kitchen and a good space for a dining-room table, and I had all mod.

cons. and constant hot water. When I stood at my front door I looked across to the Downs. To me this was heaven, and I spent four very happy years there.

Darkness and Day came out in the early summer of 1951. I wrote to Ivy saying how pleased I would be to read the book again, and I told her what I thought of the reviews. As usual I received an answer almost by return.

5, Braemar Mansions,
Cornwall Gardens. S.W.7.
June 4. 1951.

Dear Miss Greig,

Thank you very much for your letter.

I thought you could not have heard of my great trouble – the greatest I could have had, the death of Margaret Jourdain after a short illness on April 5th.

I find I can only live from day to day, and do not look forward; and concentration of any kind seems impossible. And of course I have had the manifold duties that are a part of these times.

I am glad that you like the country, and that your work progresses. I must try to get back to mine before long, but so far the effort seems too much.

I have stayed at Alfriston and liked it very much, but I always think that London offers the most as a place to *live in*, though it is a horrid place to come to for a day. I am just going into the country for three weeks, but next time you are in London I hope you will have lunch or tea with me.

I am glad to have your address, and shall need your help in future, though not yet.

Yours ever,
Ivy Compton-Burnett.

I had seen no notice of Margaret's death. My daily paper was *The Manchester Guardian*, as it called itself in those days. And at that time I knew no one in Ivy's circle who might have passed the news on to me.

I wrote at once, offering my sympathy. I thought of her words: 'I can only live from day to day.' Bereft, Ivy found herself companionless after more than thirty years of perfect companionship. Grief can't be measured, but Ivy's loss was to endure to the last syllable of her time. 'Time is not a great healer,' she had written in *Darkness and Day*. 'Sometimes it does not heal at all.' Ivy would have many friends, but no companion. I used to think of this every time I said goodbye to her. When the front door closed there would be no one in the sitting-room.

As the years passed there were days, a birthday or an anniversary they had both shared, when Ivy felt her loss more keenly. I was aware of these days and thought of them as her 'Margaret days'. On these days Margaret's name came up, inevitably, and Margaret became a kind of invisible presence between us. But she seldom spoke of her loss until the last months of her life. By that time, exhausted and frail, her defences were weakened.

Soon after the news of Margaret's death the papers gave the news that Ivy had been awarded the C.B.E. in the Birthday Honours list. I wrote at once to congratulate her, and on 21 June I had a short note of thanks. She wrote:

> I must just thank you for both your letters, and say how much I hope you will come to see me when you come to London.

Yours ever,
Ivy Compton-Burnett.

But I was not to see her until August of the following year. I went to London mostly on business, and mostly I disliked going. Also, when I was there, I thought it best not to 'bother' Ivy, though 'bother' is not quite the word to use. But for many years I had this idea that unless she sent for me to get a manuscript or to bring the typed copies, any chance visit of mine was simply an interruption in her daily routine – always a fairly full one. I learned later that I was mistaken in this. She really enjoyed having someone there to talk to, to have tea with her, to sit by the fire eating chocolates with her, or walking with her on her balcony while she cut off the dead heads, pulled out weeds, or simply looked at her show of flowers. On 2 July 1952, I received the good news that she had written another novel.

> Would you be able to type a short novel for me fairly soon? If so I will send it to you. I have hoped that you would come to luncheon or tea with me one day when you were in London.

Ivy Compton-Burnett

She was obviously rather hurt by my neglect of her, and now, to make matters worse, I wasn't free at that time to type her novel. I forget why, I may have been on the point of going away for a holiday.

I wrote saying I would be back at the end of the month. I told her I had been unable to get the usual paper she liked, and I asked her if she would like to tell Barkers to send me a ream, as that is where I always got it, and I knew she shopped there. Later, as I knew her better, I would never have dreamt of asking her this, and of course I could get paper in Eastbourne or Brighton. Ivy's answer was characteristic.

> 5, Braemar Mansions,
> Cornwall Gardens,
> S.W.7.
> July 6th. 1952.

Dear Miss Greig,

Thank you so much for your letter.

I will send the MS. to you at the end of July, when you will be able to cope with it. And in the meantime I am sending you a cheque for £7 so that you can order the paper yourself, in case I make a mistake in it.

I shall want a carbon copy.

Last time your machine made phantom question marks at the end of sentences, and the printer sometimes put them in. Perhaps this could be obviated. We can settle the balance of the account when the work is done.

I am so glad you like your new life, and that your work is congenial to you. I don't think pace matters.

> Yours ever,
> Ivy Compton-Burnett

I had often complained to her that I wrote at a snail's pace. The 'phantom question mark' was a mystery until the next time I typed. I found then that if I went too near the edge of the paper at the end of a line and had to get a full-stop in, the full-stop was smudged.

On 24 July Ivy wrote again telling me she had sent the manuscript by registered post. This was the novel *The Present and the Past*. I finished typing it by the middle of August. As usual, I enjoyed typing it, and wrote telling her so, and how each new book of hers was truly 'a happy event'. I wrote briefly about it, and what I said must have pleased her. She wrote:

> Thank you *so* much for your letter. Will you come to lunch with me on Saturday, August 23rd. at 1? My afternoon is gone.
>
> I. C-B.

It was at this lunch, I remember, that I introduced the subject of the Beatnik world to her. This was done half mischievously, I am afraid, from a curiosity to hear her comments on a world beyond – far, far beyond, her ivory tower. I didn't know much about the Beatnik world myself. I had read a book called *The Holy Barbarians* by Laurence Lipton about this time. It was an account of the Beat world of poets and artists in San Francisco. It had made a great impression on me. When I lived in London I had gone to poetry readings in pubs, and remember going to one in Dulwich with a group that included Muriel Spark – who had not then become a novelist – and other young and promising writers. The Beat movement at that time, in the early fifties, was a revival, a sign of enthusiasm, of promise, a sort of resurrection after the dreary war and post-war period. And I held forth to Ivy, for a minute or two, on the brave new world that had such people in it. One quotes poor old Queen Victoria too often, but Ivy was just as icily unamused. She was quite unable, she said, to take any interest in people of that kind, and she was sure none of her friends could know about them, or want to know about them. On these occasions, when I tried to open a small window in that cabined and confined world of hers, and she promptly slammed it shut, I never argued with her, and we managed to change the subject quite smoothly. One learned to come to terms with what I can only call the strange dichotomy of her mind and personality. Because on the one hand there was the brilliant novelist, and the scholar, wise, witty and a most profound student of human nature, and on the other, someone who could show a pathetic and surprising helplessness when a crisis occurred, someone really ignorant of a great part of contemporary life. It seemed here that at such times Margaret Jourdain took over. When she died Ivy, bereft, often floundered.

'She did so many things I find difficult to do – like doing up a parcel for instance,' Ivy told me after lunch, pointing to an arrangement of brown paper and string she had been struggling with when I arrived. The doctor who had attended Margaret in her last illness, Stephen Pasmore, a family friend of ours, had told me how surprised he was that someone as brilliant as Ivy could be so helpless at such a time. Her helplessness was truly pitiful in a crisis – in 1963, for instance, when her landlord told her he wanted her flat and she would have to find other accommodation. This helplessness caused her needless suffering, but it never quenched the vital spark that was the real Ivy. When the dilemma was solved and the danger over and she was once more at peace with herself, she got on with her writing and her entertaining, wise, witty, classic as ever. As Clemence says in *Two Worlds and their Ways*: 'That is another thing you learn, to know what you know.' Ivy knew what she knew. All the rest was irrelevant.

Having lunch with Ivy when she had just finished a novel, and having lunch with her when I had just finished typing it, were two quite different experiences, and this was something I had to learn to know. I had to choose safe subjects of talk in the first event, for having just finished a novel could leave her drained and irritable. My new way of life in the country was always a safe topic. It was usually her first question when I arrived: 'Well, do you still enjoy living in the country?'

And of course I did still enjoy it. I am a country lover. But if she had just finished a novel I told her how stimulating I found London; I would go to a gallery, I said, or to a concert, or a theatre. I would tell her what I loved about living in the country when I brought the typed novel to her. I loved the quiet, I told her.

'It's quiet here,' she said. 'You might really be in the country here.'

Yes, that was true. But one was soon out of the quiet.

'Well, you go to Eastbourne and Brighton for your shopping. No town is quiet.'

Ivy would have the last word.

Books were a safe subject and one that interested us both. On the whole we had the same tastes where modern novelists were concerned. I made the mistake of telling her, in a letter, that I had laughed out loud when reading *Lucky Jim*. Ivy told me that she had got it out from Harrods library.

'It isn't my book,' she reported. 'Not my book at all.'

I thought she would not like Salinger's *The Catcher in the Rye* but I always reported my reading to her, and I told her how much I had enjoyed this book. To my surprise she had read it, and enjoyed it, and now spoke of it with enthusiasm.

'Such a clever study of a boy,' she said. 'Such a very clever study.'

She read Mary McCarthy, but disliked what she called 'the messiness' of her later novels.

'If one wants all those physical details,' she said, 'one would go to medical books for them.'

When Hemingway died, and we both recalled our different pleasures in his different books, Ivy recommended his advice on style. He gives this in his autobiography, and I looked it up.

'All you have to do is to write one true sentence. Write the truest that you know.'

Remembering Ivy's strongly shaped sentences, this acknowledgement to the master of the stark and compact style was especially interesting.

Henry James was almost a closed subject between us. She disliked any reference to her writing as being in the Henry James tradition, which it was not. He was not her author – and he *was* mine – and she always said she had not read enough of him to be at all influenced by him.

In interviews, and to me, she always declared that Charlotte Brontë wrote better novels than Emily. She liked the firmer construction, and the related parts of the novel as Charlotte wrote them. Jane Austen was her great favourite. Her brief dismissal of E. M. Forster in an interview is well known. 'Haven't we over-rated him?'

I remember in a discussion we had I said I looked for anguish from such writers as Hardy and James and Emily Brontë and Meredith, and that this was a mark of their greatness, and we talked of Shakespearean tragedy in this connection. And I said thank heavens that, once in a hundred years, we have a classic writer whose vision is cool, circumspect, amused, cynical and witty, and I thought this gift was rarer.

The Present and the Past was the first novel Ivy wrote after Margaret's death. Ivy always declared that nothing had happened in her life. When she was asked to write a biographical note to a Penguin edition of one of her novels she wrote: 'I have had such an uneventful life that there is nothing to say.'

Was she looking back on her life with Margaret when Elton Scrope says: 'We have had such a dear little narrow life. I could not bear a wealth of experience?'

The talk between Elton and Ursula Scrope, brother and sister, and the talk of the servants are the best things in this novel. The present and the past meet when Catherine, Cassius Clare's first wife returns to the neighbourhood and meets her successor, Flavia. In one scene the two wives and Elton and Ursula discuss the subject of being average.

'Do we all regard ourselves as above the average?' (says Catherine.)
'Well, think what the average is,' said Elton.
'That hardly matters,' said Flavia, 'as everyone seems to be above it. Can you think of an average person?'
'Well, I would rather not think of one,' said Ursula.

63

'Most people must be average,' said Catherine, 'or there would be no such thing.'

'Well, let us hope there is not,' said her sister.

'I find them pleasant to look at, pleasant to listen to, pleasant in themselves.'

'I am sure they are, but I do not find them so.'

This passage of dialogue is typically Ivy's, but as I typed it I wondered if Ivy was remembering an extraordinary conversation that took place in the Woolf's home in Sussex many years before: Virginia had died some ten years before this novel was written. The particular conversation is one that is remembered today in 1970: it began by Virginia, who could sometimes be cruel, pouncing on an unfortunate 'average' visitor – *not* one of the 'Bloomsberries' – with the command: 'Now, do tell us, what is it like to be ordinary?'

Ivy was certainly not present on that occasion, but she may have heard of it from her friend Vita Sackville-West, Virginia's cousin. It was never Ivy's habit to note down such scraps of conversation, to be used later. In an interview once she was asked about this, and was told that Katherine Mansfield had always kept such notes and used them later, and Ivy had made the comment: 'Well, I should have thought she *hadn't* used them.'

The novel has less of this quick tennis-play of words and ideas – as in a Lyly comedy – than her other novels, – *Elders and Betters* and *Mother and Son*, for instance, to mention only two. It struck me as being a little thin in content with rather too many long-winded speeches from Cassius Clare, one of Ivy's less formidable tyrants, and too much talk from her three-year-old. Ivy's children were of the period when parents like them to be seen and not heard, but they all had their word to say in these novels, and they said it.

Henry and Megan, aged eight and seven, discuss the problems involved in having both a mother and a stepmother.

'It seems best to have your own mother all the time, or not to have her at all,' said Megan.

'Having two takes all your thought,' said Henry, 'so that you don't have any over for your own life.'

'I am afraid you see the truth,' said his mother.

'Truth has to be seen when it alters everything,' (said Henry.)

And, as usual, Ivy's servants can quote poetry. Here the housemaid, Madge, quotes Marvell, and the others, Ainger, the butler, Mrs Frost, the cook – whose dry remarks are among the best things in the book – and Kate, another maid, all show their familiarity with the poem. Only Simon, the boy, is ignorant. Their talk has been of Cassius Clare's pretence at suicide.

'Well, I must admit to a sense of disappointment.'
'Ah, you wanted to hear of incidents, Kate.'
'It would have been nice,' said Madge.
'But I should have been called upon to witness them,' said Ainger. 'And that would not have been so. To see people of calibre fall from their level! But I was to be spared.'
'I hoped to be called upon to hear of them,' said Madge. 'I wish they had something common done or mean, upon that memorable scene.'
'The words apply, Madge,' said Ainger.
'Who was it who did nothing common or mean?' said Simon.
'It was only once that it was anyone,' said Mrs Frost.
'Someone who was to be beheaded,' said Kate. 'It would be hard to be oneself then.'
'Anyhow for long,' said Mrs Frost.
'It was Charles the First of England,' said Ainger. 'Charles, our Royalist king.'

And here is a sentence with that particular Ivyish balance.

'Mr Clare saw his son as he was, and kept his feeling for him, and Flavia seemed to fear to do the one, in case she should cease to do the other.'

Such a sentence is bliss to type. And towards the end of the novel there is a memorable sentence where Ivy conveys Flavia's grief and bitter loss in an unusual way. Catherine (the first wife) is taking her own two sons from Flavia who has brought them up as her own. Catherine says:

'Do you not see the further time? When you will have your children by themselves, without those of another woman? As it is natural for you to have them. As it is natural for you to be seen with them. Is there not, will there not be, a recompense there?'
Flavia looked into her face, and there seemed to be a third presence in the hall, the difference between them.

I never heard Ivy make a remark that she had already used in one of her novels until a few weeks before her death. In this novel, *The Present and the Past*, Madge (the maid) says:

'We have to be thankful for small mercies.'
'I am not,' said Mrs Frost. 'They are too small.'

In the summer of 1969 I was out on the balcony with Ivy, and as she turned to go into the sitting-room, I asked if I could help her.

'No thank-you,' she said. 'I can manage very well with this –' (her support). 'I must be thankful for small mercies. But of course when they are too small . . .'

She looked at me, her eyes alight with amusement.

Ivy finished her next novel *Mother and Son* in June 1954. June was her birthday month. She was 69. I heard from her on the 10th and 12th of that month as we were unable to fix a day for our usual meeting. Finally I heard on the 22nd. Of the manuscript she wrote:

> It is short, but it will want some care, as it is rather smudged and interrupted by interpolations. If it takes more than the average time you must let me know.
>
> I am going away on Monday, and if I may have the typed copies (1 carbon as usual) by July 20th. it will do quite well. Perhaps I shall see you when you bring it.
>
> I hope you still like your country life, and are well.
>
> Yours ever,
>
> Ivy Compton-Burnett.

Mother and Son was a novel I most enjoyed typing, and I have read it since more than once. It is strongly melodramatic in parts, with an Elizabethan flavour, in Hester's open villainy, for instance, her scheming and her eavesdropping, and the fact that she is not all bad. The three children are the 'chorus', and especially towards the end of the novel their comments form those interpolations needed by Ivy to fill out the book. I thought, when I typed the book, that Adrian cried too often. Not that Ivy would have written 'he cried'. 'Adrian broke into weeping' was her way of describing a child's grief. She preferred the phrase to the bare statement. When an older child cries she 'sank into tears'. When they laughed 'they broke into mirth'. And Roseberry is described as 'going into mirth'. Hester does not look at Mr Hume, a widower she sees as a possible husband for herself, she 'threw her eyes over his face', and in another place, when she is angry with him, she speaks 'flashing her eyes over his face', both phrases carrying more weight than the bare verb. A typical phrase occurs in *Elders and Betters* when Esmond, kicks his younger brother: '. . . he lifted his foot and gave him a blow', a phrase of Cranford gentility.

Ivy's tyrant in this novel is the mother, Miranda Hume, a woman of

66

eighty-seven. The book does not open with the usual breakfast scene. Miranda is about to interview a possible companion. The woman arrives and the maid announces her arrival as maids still announce such people to-day.

'The person has arrived, Ma'am.'
'What person?' said Mrs Hume.
'The person who was expected, ma'am.
'And who was expecting her?'
'I supposed it was yourself, ma'am. It would be the assumption.'
'And how would you refer to someone I was expecting?'
'I understood she was to be under consideration, ma'am.'

Ivy's old servants all have great dignity: only the young ones are crude and questioning, the socialists of the future. When I fetched the manuscript of *Mother and Son* Ivy was having staff troubles of her own, and had been interviewing women 'under consideration'. They came from an agency, and I often wondered how the interviews were conducted. This is how Miranda Hume conducted hers. After telling her husband, her son and her three grandchildren that they may stay in the room – ' . . you children keep to your side of the room and appear to be occupied.'

'It is good of you to come to see an old woman and to think of being her companion. Will you tell me in what ways you are suited to such a post?'
'I am companionable,' said Miss Burke, hesitating in spite of the appositeness of her claim. 'And I am interested in other people and their lives.'
Miranda's face showed that something confirmed her expectations.
'What is your age?'
'I beg your pardon, Mrs Hume?'
'How old are you? How many years have you lived?'
'I am over thirty, Mrs Hume.'
'Yes, so I see. So am I. By how much are you over it?'
'I did not expect to be asked my age.'
'I am under no obligation to consider that.'
'I am not much under forty,' said Miss Burke, changing her tone under Miranda's eye. 'I am actually forty-seven.'
'You would pass for less. You could say you were forty-two. It comes of the easy life of a companion.'

The inquisition goes on for two more pages, punctuated by 'sounds of mirth' from the corners of the room. Miranda asks:

'Have you a good voice for reading aloud?'

'It could hardly be different from my ordinary voice.'

'Would you read as if you had written the books yourself, and felt self-conscious about them?'

'No, I should only try to interpret them.'

'You cannot just read simply and clearly what is before your eyes?' said Miranda, giving a sigh.

'Yes, if that is what you want.'

'Well, it naturally is. Why should I wish for your implied opinion? I could ask you for that.'

'Well, I would remember that.'

'And you would not sit as if you had a host of unspoken thoughts seething within you?'

'It is not likely I should have a host of them.'

'Or as if your mind were a blank?'

'I would try to strike the mean.'

'I have no liking for smart answers.'

The bullying tone has Brontë echoes. But the differences between the earlier and the later novelist are wide: the former was herself a victim – I am thinking chiefly of Charlotte. And the victim of her stories triumphs. She is the heroine. Ivy, on the other hand, though not a bully, was an autocrat, and held all the weapons wherewith to quell. Her bullies triumph. Ivy is on the side of power; Charlotte on the side of virtue.

There is much comedy in this novel. Ivy had met my cat Prunella for a fleeting moment and declared herself to be quite intolerant of the creatures. But there was never any conversation between us then, or at any time. Emma Greatheart, one of Ivy's most delightful characters, and her friend Hester Wolsey have discussions with their housekeeper about their cat, one or two of these being 'interpolations'. The house-keeper is the Miss Burke that did not suit Miranda Hume. Like Ivy she dislikes cats and pushes him off her lap when he springs on to it.

'Why do you call him Plautus?' said Miss Burke.

'Oh, because he *is* Plautus,' said Miss Wolsey. 'Because the essence oι Plautus is in him. How could he be called anything else?'

'Who was Plautus in real life?'

'Who could he have been but the person to give this Plautus his name?'

'He was a Latin writer,' said Miss Greatheart, as Miss Burke left a second question unanswered. 'I think he wrote plays; not very good ones.'

'Why did you call the cat after him?'

'Well, he has not written any good plays either,' said Miss Wolsey . ..

Ivy, like Shakespeare, has her clowns, and this is a novel where comic relief is needed. There are passages of murk and melodrama. When Miranda feels, suddenly, that her last hour is come, her husband, Julius seizes this opportunity to tell her of the years in their married life when he was unfaithful and had three children by his mistress. Miranda's answer to that is to quote Macbeth:

'And all our yesterdays have lighted fools the way to dusty death. This is what mine have done for me. This is what I have, a dead marriage, now to end in death.'

She dies upon the instant, and Hester Wolsey, overhearing, enters, seeing her chance.

This is melodrama, but 'Ivyish' melodrama, its roots in Greek tragedy, and Greek tragedy in nineteenth-century dress becomes inevitably melodrama. Some of Hardy's tragic scenes suffer the same fate; Ivy bore a greater burden of inheritance from the Elizabethans, of comedy as well as tragedy. The former follows close on the heels of the latter, but the comedy itself is not Plautian but Congreve and Wilde.

And to digress for a moment: the term 'Ivyish' came into use about this time. Reviewers would comment on a book's title as being 'Ivyish', and Ivy herself rather enjoyed the compliment.

'Like "Shakesperian",' I said.

She was very modest about her gifts and would quickly turn the compliment aside by saying: 'But it was sheer plagiarism calling his book *Brothers and Sisters*, sheer plagiarism.'

I remember once telling her of an incident Nancy Spain described in one of her books, an account of her first years as a writer.

'Who,' Ivy demanded, 'is Nancy Spain?'

I told her she wrote thrillers. 'And she went to a publisher's party, not knowing anyone there except Elizabeth Bowen ...'

'Did *she* know this person?' Ivy asked, astonished that a friend of hers should know a writer of thrillers.

'Well, only because they both come from the same part of Ireland. Anyway, she heard Elizabeth saying to some woman writer she didn't know: "It's really too bad of Cyril to say that Ivy is the only one of us all that will live." And she had no idea who Cyril was and who Ivy was.'

Ivy liked this story; she made no comment, but her eyes lit up with laughter.

Emma Greatheart's lunch party in this novel must be one of the most amusing scenes in fiction. And though it is high comedy there are also heard the first warning rumblings of the melodrama to follow. But it is a novel where no crimes are committed, no wills are tampered with, no one is murdered. Unfaithfulness is revealed, and there is the usual 'that man's father is my father's son' sort of tangle in the Hume family.

I finished typing the novel in July in good time for her to have before she set off. She was going to Kent – I didn't ask where, it could have been to the Harold Nicolsons as she knew Vita Sackville-West well. She would sit in the garden, she told me, and correct her novel and be left in peace to work. Then she would return, refreshed, and slowly turn over ideas for her next book.

When I visited her in between books I always gave a quick look about the room hoping to see one of those blue or red exercise books. Sometimes she asked me to fetch something from her bedroom, or a vase from the kitchen or a bowl from the dining-room for flowers and fruit, but I never saw the usual paraphernalia of a writer lying about in any room. And when Margaret was alive one would never suspect that two writers lived in the flat and often wrote in the same sitting-room. I think Ivy slipped her exercise books in her desk if she heard the doorbell or was expecting a visitor. And the only time I saw her reading from her own manuscript was shortly before her death. But after her death the executors had to search for it. It was under a cushion.

About this time I wrote asking her if it was possible to have one of the manuscripts I had typed, a rather naïve request on my part. I also wanted to read *Dolores*, the only novel of hers I had not read. It was not possible to buy the book, and I bethought me of the time when she had offered me any of her books, those unsold copies she kept in the cupboard in the dining-room.

My request obviously did not please Ivy, and I received a brief negative from her.

'I am so sorry but I always sell my MSS to H. Hill. And I have no copy of my early book. But it has not any great interest. I have no idea when M and S. will appear. I hope your work goes well.

I. C-B.

I never asked her about *Dolores* again; it was the one book of hers she preferred to forget. She told me some time later that Hill gave her

£20 for her manuscripts. Before she realised they were saleable she always destroyed them.

Mother and Son appeared in February 1955, about the same time as a book by Robert Liddell: *The Novels of I. Compton-Burnett*. Later, *Mother and Son* was awarded the James Tait Black Memorial Prize. Many years later, a year or two before she died, the novel came out in a paperback edition (Panther, 5s. then). A short-list review of new paperbacks appeared in one of the papers. Of *Mother and Son* the reviewer wrote: 'Typically chill, claustrophobic Compton-Burnett, with the feeling of suffocation enhanced by the near pedantic formal style. Mother fixation in the Hume family leads to intrigue and exploitation in a sequence of grim tableaux. Economical, frightening, ruthless.'

Such horrified reviewing of a novel like *Mother and Son*, a novel with really glittering comic scenes, amazes one until one remembers that Ivy makes demands on her readers which many resent. I should say, for instance, that she demands a certain level of education from her readers; and this is true of other novelists of our time, novelists like Huxley and Waugh and Rose Macaulay, to mention only three. Her books also demand an ear sensitive to the cadences of her writing, and this is true of the writing of Virginia Woolf and Elizabeth Bowen. She is not the only one to make demands on a reader. But over and above these is her demand on our powers of concentration. Either you are held from the first page to the last, or the whole thing is an effort. In a short monograph on Ivy published some time in the 1950s by the British Council Pamela Hansford Johnson declared that if one's attention strayed for a moment 'the whole thing becomes gibberish' – a typical piece of exaggeration Ivy's books can provoke. Another fault Ivy's critics find is her not, sometimes, naming the speaker so that when the dialogue is quick and the remarks short one has sometimes to guess who said what.

It is certainly true that her books provoke those who have tried to struggle through them to the most angry-sounding adjectives – grim, pedantic and claustrophobic. Her plots are grim, her style pedantic. And claustrophobic?

'If only she would describe the scenery, the countryside, and get out of her horrid dining-rooms . . .' someone protested to me, looking back in anger at a Compton-Burnett she had tried to read.

But surely the view from Ivy's dining-room windows is wide

enough. She gives us, without mentioning any names, glimpses of some formidable Victorian characters in this passage from *A House and its Head*, to take just one example. It is breakfast time on Christmas morning.

'What is that book, Grant?'
Grant uttered the title of a scientific work inimical to the faith of the day.
'Did you remember that I refused to give it to you?'
'Yes, Uncle. That is why I asked somebody else.'
'Did you say I had forbidden it in the house?'
'No, or I should not have been given it.'
Duncan took the book, and walking to the fire, placed it upon the flames.
'Oh, Father, really!' said Nance.
'Really? Yes, really, Nance. I shall really do my best to guide you – to force you, if it must be, into the way you must go. I would not face the consequences of doing otherwise.'

Such a quotation from *A House and its Head* looks out into the world of Darwin and the Barretts of Wimpole Street and Samuel Butler and Edmund Gosse, the world of tyrant fathers and rebellious youth. There is, at other breakfast scenes, the busy, sometimes prying neighbourliness that recalls Cranford and Jane Austen, the comedy of Dickens and Wilde, the melodrama of those two spinsters Edith Somerville and Martin Ross. There is no claustrophobia, Ivy makes her readers work, and we have our reward.

3

It was unfortunate that very few of my friends liked Ivy's books as she had told me she would always welcome any friend of mine. My sister enjoyed her books, and she had come with me when Margaret Jourdain was alive. In 1955 a friend declared herself to be an Ivy addict, and eager to meet her. Ivy was away most of the summer after the publication of *Mother and Son*, and I have a card from her dated 5 December thanking me for my letter; I had told her about my friend and added that any friend I brought came from love and homage, never from idle curiosity. She wrote:

'I should very much like to see you and your friend some time after this week. At the moment I am getting over a mild illness.'

Ivy had delicate health, but she lived gently, was on the whole very well served, and she lived to be 85. She hated the winters and usually suffered from at least one attack of bronchitis. She told me her legs were weak, and for some years before she died her heart was giving her trouble. She never complained to me of her health and never made a fuss. I guessed that the mild illness was probably bronchitis and wrote saying that it would be best to leave our meeting until after Christmas. I waited for a mild spell of weather and this came early in January. As Ivy had had a change of housekeepers I asked her if, for a change, she would like to come out to lunch. I told her I was a member of the National Book League in Albermarle Street and as it was fairly central perhaps she would like to come there. Ivy wrote in answer:

'I will come with great pleasure to the National Book League in Albemarle Street at 1 o'clock on Thursday, January 12th.'

I had become a member because the place was central. I belonged to no other club, and though this club was not residential it served the purpose of a country member making one day visits to town. My sister and I had had dinner there one evening before a concert at the Festival Hall. We found the food plain, well-cooked and nicely served.

There was a room where non-members 'waited', and this was very small. However, I hoped, as we had fixed a definite time, and we were all punctually minded, that there would be no waiting.

Unfortunately Ivy waited.

'It started raining, so I took a taxi. And that brought me here ten minutes too early,' she told us later.

My sister arrived soon after Ivy, and before my friend and I arrived. When my sister greeted her, Ivy, in her unpredictable way, declared she couldn't remember ever having met her before. When we arrived a few minutes before one we found the whole place crowded. There had been a lecture at 12 o'clock, I think by Veronica Wedgewood. These morning lectures were rather popular, and if I had known about them I wouldn't have chosen that day to ask Ivy to lunch. People poured out of the library and into the hall; everyone had evidently planned to stay for lunch, and many of them must have asked friends to meet them in that small waiting room.

Ivy's dignity on such occasions had a freezing quality. Of course we had booked a table, and we took our places as the large dining-room filled up and everyone greeted everyone else rather noisily.

My friend said: 'I wonder if any of your writer friends are here today.'

Ivy threw her eyes briefly over the crowded scene and shook her head with what was almost a shudder of horror.

The menu that day was disappointing; there was no chicken or turkey. I hoped Ivy would think the fare wholesome and plain. As we waited for the waitress to serve us, we discussed London's Regency buildings and architecture in general, and Margaret Jourdain's name came up. This was because we had all admired the beautiful Regency staircase in the main hall on our way down to the dining-room. Unfortunately by the time the waitress brought our dishes I was in such tremble inwardly that I said: 'I think Miss Jourdain is having the roast beef.'

Ivy accepted the dish, looked fiercely at me and said, whiplash-like: 'Will you kindly not call me Miss Jourdain.'

Her fierceness startled all of us and succeeded in bringing me at once more or less back to normal. I thought it ridiculous that a slip of the tongue should provoke such fierceness. I smiled at her, said I was so sorry, and wouldn't she like some horseradish sauce. After that, things went quite smoothly.

74

At such times Ivy's green-grey eyes could take on a fierce, cold glint, and she made me think of some of her old tyrants, Miranda Hume or Sabine Ponsonby, and I wished I had the wit, indulgence and charm of her Emma Greatheart and Juliet Cassidy so that in our exchanges I could match fierceness with wit, instead of falling back on horseradish sauce. But her fierceness, when it showed itself, and when I provoked it, was always short-lived. Any breach of normal decorum, and her standard was perhaps exceptionally high, was annoying to her, and she never failed to let this be seen. But having let it be seen, the matter was over.

Later, outside in Albemarle Street, we found a taxi for her. She would go to Harrods, to the library, to change her book, she told us. She thanked us with that courtesy that was especial to Ivy, so that we felt she could not have enjoyed herself more if we had taken her to Claridges.

It had been one of her 'Margaret days'. Margaret's name had come up very early in connection with the Regency staircase. My blunder must have been doubly painful. And I remembered, too, that she was writing again, and that this would be her fifteenth novel. Altogether a day of strain for Ivy.

In October her postcard came with the news that she had finished her new novel.

'A novel that I do not want to trust to the post,' she wrote. 'Could you come to lunch with me on October 26th. at 1. and take it back with you. I hope you are well and will be able to.'

And of course I was. I went up to London on the date she suggested and we had lunch together. She had had one or two changes of housekeepers, but was now settled with a friendly Irish woman.

'She likes to be spoken to when she opens the door to people,' Ivy told me, when we were alone in the sitting-room.

Well, fortunately, I had spoken to her. 'About the weather,' I said.

Ivy was sensitively aware of the fine, and sometimes not so fine, shades of difference between the old-time servant, the maid, the working housekeeper and the cook-general. She had had them all and I soon learned to take my cue from the greeting I was given at the front door as to how to judge the status, and whether, later, when my plate was removed for the next course, to sit in silence, or to look up with a smile and say: 'Delicious. I'm going to ask you for the recipe before I go.'

Ivy preferred the maids one could be silent with at table, I think. On the whole she was very well served, and the several changes were caused mostly by various family troubles of the women concerned, and not by any trouble with Ivy herself.

I remember at this particular lunch we had a dish that Ivy liked especially, boiled gammon with parsley sauce.

Ivy said: 'Now you've had a long journey from Sussex. Did you eat a good breakfast?'

I told her I was not a breakfast eater, not porridge or eggs, but I enjoyed my toast and butter and marmalade.

'I think one should start the day with something more solid,' she said. 'When we have ham in the house, like this, I like to have a small slice for breakfast.'

She ate very little, helping herself to tiny portions two or three times instead of taking a normal helping. She cut her food very small and was always busily occupied with it, mincing it up, slicing up a boiled potato, taking tiny helpings of parsley sauce, and at the same time discussing the books or the plays we were all reading or seeing at that time.

I never discussed her new novel with her, though we often spoke in a general way of writing, and especially of new novels, and of reviews and reviewers. I never questioned her on her methods – she had told me where she wrote her novels – 'in one or other of the armchairs' – and I had told her many times how much I enjoyed typing her novels, and reading them later. I knew most of the answers as to how she set about writing a new novel because she regularly submitted herself to press interviews. She was frank about her liking for plots and the period she chose. The famous conversation with Margaret Jourdain published in *Orion* (1945), revealed all that needed revealing as to her method and her thoughts about writing. Her often quoted statements in that conversation: 'I do not feel that I have any real or organic knowledge of life later than about 1910', and '. . . as regards plots I find real life no help at all. Real life seems to have no plots, and as I think a plot desirable and almost necessary, I have this extra grudge against life . . .' these statements tell us everything we need to know about her reason for writing as she did. But I sometimes wondered about this 'real life' that 'seemed to have no plots', when she admitted knowing nothing of life later than 1910. The life we each of us lead is 'real' to us, and Ivy's life was certainly too confined for plots other than the ones she invented. But she read the papers. However, though I might think about this while we ate our boiled gammon and parsley sauce, followed by a mousse, or fruit and cream and a baked custard, I never questioned her about these statements of hers, especially when she had just finished a book.

'. . . It is the exhaustion after a prolonged effort,' Ada Merton tells her father, a serious academic writer when he declares himself to be conscious of failure after finishing a book. When Hereward Egerton, a writer of popular books, and his sister Zillah are announced, Ada says:

'Now you have come at an opportune moment . . . You find my father out of heart, and can say a word to cheer him. You can be no strangers to the reaction after endeavour.'

And Hereward answers:

'. . . Reaction may not come of itself. It tends to carry a sense of unsuccess . . . I can offer nothing better than sympathy.'

These quotations are from *A God and his Gifts* (1963), the last novel published in her life. When I read them I was reminded of those different meetings between us, those when she had just finished a novel, and 'felt drained', and our meetings when I had finished typing it, or when the novel was published.

After lunch we had coffee in the sitting-room before the fire, and there was a box with chocolates in it between us. Ivy liked chocolates, and her friends brought them to her so that whenever I went there were always chocolates on the table. She had a box she used for left-overs from other boxes. She disliked too many odds and ends about the place and would throw away a box that was nearly empty after tipping the chocolates into this other box. It meant that the chocolates were a mixed lot, and loose instead of in neat rows. While we sipped our coffee and discussed Simone de Beauvoir's latest book, Ivy rummaged about the box, her small hands busily turning over the chocolates this way and that, pushing some to one side and some to the other. I have this vivid mental picture of her doing this, turning the chocolates this way and that. Was it something to do with her nervous condition at the time, I wondered, or was she looking for a special kind?

'Have another chocolate,' she said. 'On the whole I don't really care for modern French novels.'

'In and out of bed,' I said, taking a chocolate.

'In and out of bed,' she agreed.

Her fingers closed on a peppermint cream, paper-wrapped. I hadn't seen it. If I had I would have taken it instead of the chocolate. I have a weakness for peppermint creams. But Ivy peered at the thing as at an unidentifiable object, something she had never seen before, turning it this way and that, her expression blank with bewilderment. What was it doing there, the vulgar thing? After a full minute of concentrated examination she flung it on the fire. I nearly choked. It must have seemed like a bit of that 'real life' she had a grudge against. Her action was typical, it was 'Ivyish'. And if I had laughed outright at her for chucking a sweet away because it was not a chocolate she would have told me, I think, that it wasn't the kind of sweet one would want.

The novel I took down to Sussex to type was called *A Father and his Fate*. There is less action in it than in earlier novels, and this is true of most of her later books. The tyrant is Miles Mowbray, on the whole a benevolent one. I think Shakespeare was the presence that hovered closest to Ivy when she wrote this novel. Miles turns Lear-like, demanding proofs of his daughters' devotion, calling his youngest his Cordelia. Believing his wife has been drowned he decides to marry his adopted son's fiancee Verena. Meanwhile his wife's place in the dining-room remains empty.

'Perhaps Aunt Ellen's ghost is in the place,' Malcolm says.

'Or will be when Verena comes to it. It is a Shakespearean state of affairs.'

The characters in Ivy's novels frequently see themselves as playing a part, like actors in a play, and her books are made up of a series of dramatic scenes broken by those interludes when the chorus comments on the action. Ivy's plots, like Shakespeare's are all highly improbable. This plot is one of the most improbable. But it is amusing. The sea casts up Miles's wife and Verena marries the son instead of the father. Bedroom furniture is moved around, and some nightclothes of Verena's are found

... thrown anyhow into the drawers, and unthought of since. They were of a kind to be chosen for an occasion, were marked with her name, and had been in use.'

leaving no doubt that Verena and Miles had slept together.

'We shall say nothing about it, Uncle.'

Miles's nephews assure him, and return to their home to recount it all to their mother's companion. But before they go Miles has his word to say:

'I did what I could for myself, because I had to . . . And because no one else thought of doing anything. I thought of other people more than they thought of me. I look back and see that I did. And few of us can say as much.'

'Everything is in order now,' (says Miss Gibbon, the housekeeper). 'If someone will shut the drawers.'

Something must have delayed my typing of *A Father and his Fate* because I have a postcard from Ivy dated 14th November 1956 in answer to one from me. She wrote:

'Nov. 28th. will do quite well for the book. I am so glad you enjoyed it. But will not you and your friend come to lunch or tea on Wednesday 28th? I do not know your plans.

It wd. amuse me if you wd. pinch off a flower from each of your three balsams and post them to me in an envelope. I only want one myself, but wd. like to see the other colours and see if mine is different. Let me know about 28th.

Thank you so much.

I. C-B.

I remember her balsam very well, a beautiful pink one with a fine branching way. It grew tall and was kept on the floor by the sitting-room window. Ivy was very fond of it. I had three of these 'Busy Lizzies' and must have told Ivy that one of them was a much deeper pink, almost a coral shade. I forget about posting the blossoms. I know when I saw her her balsam had died – 'quite suddenly, no one knows why.'

The friend she speaks of was the one she met at the not very successful Albemarle Street lunch, and she very much wanted to meet Ivy 'at home', and had asked me if I could arrange this. I told her that we had been asked to tea, and warned her that it was not an easy meal, but that as it was late for cucumbers it might not be too difficult. I threw this at her on the 'phone and just before the pips went, and she had no idea what I was talking about. However, all was well, and it seems I had had the last of those cucumber and lettuce and cream cheese teas. While we waited for Ivy in the sitting-room, and my friend looked about her I quickly saw that there was no table laid for tea. Then Ivy appeared and greeted us, and a bell rang and we went to the dining-room where a normal tea with bread and butter and cake awaited us. I don't know when Ivy made this change as I had not had tea with her since I left London. After this visit with my friend I was to have tea with her many times in this dining-room, or before the sitting-room fire with the tea-trolley between us when it was the maid's day off, and tea remained normal, no cucumber.

On this November afternoon with the three of us at her tea table, everything went well. We had found some charming Garnet roses to bring her and before tea I had put them in a vase – not a happy task in that flat as Ivy's vases were tall and narrow and I enjoyed arranging flowers. But the roses pleased her as flowers always pleased her.

I had now heard definitely that Curtis Brown had not been able to get my book published. It had had good reports, Spencer Curtis Brown told me, but in the final judgment it was always voted a non-seller. We talked about non-sellers and publishers' worries and Ivy said that she and Margaret had both been non-sellers. Now, however, she was pleased to tell us that *Manservant and Maidservant* was to be broadcast. Ivy liked Beatrix Lehmann to play the parts of her elderly women tyrants, but there would be no part for her in *Manservant and Maidservant*, nor, for that matter in the two novels Ivy was still to publish, after *A Father and his Fate*. But Beatrix Lehmann would have made a wonderful Jocasta, the fierce old grandmother in Ivy's last and unfinished novel. We spoke of the theatre; Ivy and I had seen *The Innocents*, the play based on Henry James's *Turn of the Screw*, and I think it was about now that Priestly's adaptation of Iris Murdoch's *The Severed Head* was showing.

Ivy was so especially kind to one's friends that I always wished more of mine liked her books because to me Ivy and her books were inseparable. If you loved one you loved the other, and you understood Ivy from reading her books and enjoyed her books more for having met her. I suppose one could say this of most authors, but it was especially true of Ivy.

I wrote to thank her for letting me bring my friend to tea, and I received a note in answer, dated 7 December 1956.

So many thanks for your letter and the nicely typed book. I liked seeing you very much. The little red roses are still here and happy.

Ivy C-B.

During the following year we were to meet as I had to go to London in October. When I got to town, however, I found I had shingles, and though I kept my other appointment I dare not go near Ivy. I sent her a message and went home. Ivy wrote on 31 October 1957:

> I am so sorry for the news, and hope I shall see you here before long. Mind you take care. Shingles is a rather lingering thing, and can't be hurried.
>
> Ivy C-B.

A year later, 2 November 1958, she was writing to tell me she had finished another novel, just under two years since I had finished the typing of *A Father and his Fate*, not bad going for someone in her seventy-fifth year. She often said that once she 'got going' on another novel she got on with it fairly quickly, but she could be a year in between books when she wrote nothing. I don't think Ivy was ever in a hurry to finish a book, but she can cover the ground more quickly by letting her bores have their heads. Here is a typical speech – spoken by Cassius Clare in *The Present and the Past*.

> 'Well, I can't help it, can I? I am sure I cannot solve them. I shall just let things take their course. And if you are guided by me you will do the same. And you are guided by me more often than you think, Flavia. I am not such a nonentity in my own house. I often find my influence working and having its result. Though no one would acknowledge it. Oh, no, I should not expect that. But it remains that I am the head of the family and that must mean something. Take the example of this last decision. Who really made it, you or I?'

Such speeches are rare: it is Ivy letting the reins go slack. Talk of this kind sharpens our appetite for the stronger, more taut sentences, the drier and witty comments. Jane Austen uses the same method.

I was glad to have Ivy's card in November, 1958, with the news of another novel. She wrote:

> I hope you are well after this long time. Could you come to luncheon with me on Tuesday, November 11th. at 1, and take back a short book to be typed? I should like to see you apart from this purpose.
>
> Ivy Compton-Burnett

The novel I fetched was *A Heritage and its History*, Ivy's sixteenth novel. It is a short book, but by this time I was fairly immersed in country life – I often told Ivy one can be far busier in a country village than in London – and I had a part-time job in Eastbourne. My aim was to get it done before the Christmas rush, but I couldn't manage this. I had to write and tell her I could not come up to town before Christmas, and posting the typescript was out of the question. Ivy, patient as ever, sent a note back: 'Early January will do quite well.'

It was not a difficult novel to type, and I thought it one of her best. There are many beautiful passages where poetry and prose draw together – Julia's speech for instance which I have quoted earlier. And there is good, sharp dialogue:

'To say openly what is to be said! Ah, how much braver and better!'

'I think it is much worse. I can't tell you how bad it seems to me. And I never admire courage. It is always used against people. What other purpose has it?'

'I have said what I had to say. I shall not add another word.'

'I hope not, unless you mince it,' said Fanny.

It is a novel with such good dramatic situations in it that it is not surprising Julian Mitchell was able to dramatise it. And of course Ivy's gift for a dramatic situation need not be emphasised. She was a regular theatregoer until the last years of her life, and she thought of her books as something between plays and novels. I think if one were asked to point to a quotation that best accounted for her method and all the fabric of her vision it would be to Jacques's well-worn speech:

'All the world's a stage, And all the men and women merely players;'

'We seem to be living in a play,' Anne says, in *Darkness and Day*. 'And so we are,' said Mildred. 'And so is everyone else. What else does anyone do?'

And in *A Heritage and its History*:

'That should have been in a play,' said Walter, 'with the audience knowing the truth.'

The truth in this case being that Rhoda's baby son is really Simon's child and not her husband's. Later, when the truth has been broken to the family, and Hamish finds that the girl he wants to marry is really his sister, Walter again makes his comment:

'I wish Shakespeare was here,' said Walter, to break the tension. 'I mean, I wish I was he. If I was I could make so much of the scene. It is sad it has to be wasted.'

'Can you bring it to an end?' said Simon.

'He would have done so. And it is not the easiest part.'

Calendars are produced every year with Patience Strong's sayings. I think I should like to see Ivy's sentences – a different one every day, and several would come from this novel.

'It is in our minds that we live much of our life,' Rhoda says. And 'Words are all we have. It is no good to find fault with them' (Hamish). And when Hamish dies Julia says: 'To live is nothing but wishing. It is always too late.'

A Heritage and its History came out later that year (1959). There is a gap in our correspondence; I have no card or letter from her until 24 December 1960. I always sent her a Christmas card, and I must have sent a letter with it. She writes:

'It was so nice to hear from you and know your news. I have often thought of you. I am glad you are *writing and not working*, as I find people put it!!

I am trying to finish a book and hope to ask you to type it before long. But do come to see me when you come to London. I am so often at home. Just give me a little choice of day and time. And my love and thanks.

I. C-B.

One of the mistakes I made in my long relationship with Ivy was my fear of 'being a nuisance', of interrupting her work – 'I get many interruptions,' she often told me when I asked her if she was writing. I could have seen her more often, especially in the last years of her life when I spent two or three months a year in London. Until the sixties we met at most twice a year. This meant that every meeting imposed a certain strain – for me, perhaps for her. There is a rough friendship in country life, easy and warm and uncomplicated. And on my rare visits to London there were happy reunions with old friends with the 'My dear, simply ages since we met. I've heaps to tell you' . . . sort of greeting, and one talked for hours. But visiting Ivy was rather like visiting a Reverend Mother in a convent. I used to put on a hat and gloves for my visit long after I normally left off both. One had to make a time with her housekeeper. One had to break ice again after the first greeting, though really there was no ice. There was only my shyness and her quiet dignity. Later, when I was in London for longer periods our relationship was an easier one.

Ivy had many friends, but in her last years she missed her old friends, friends she had known for thirty or forty years, friends who had known Margaret Jourdain – Rose Macaulay, Una Pope-Hennessey, Ernest

83

Thesiger, Vita Sackville-West, Theodora Benson – she often spoke of them to me and of the blank they left. And there were many others. It was fortunate that the urge to write remained, and her lively interest in people, the great pleasure she had in entertaining them, especially round her table at tea-time. 'So many people nowadays do not take afternoon tea. I think that is very bad,' she told W. J. Weatherby when he interviewed her for *The Guardian* in 1962.

She finished the book she was working on and sent me a card dated 10 February 1961.

> Would you be able to come to lunch on Wednesday, February 15th. at 1, and take my MS, and, if possible, type it at once? I very much hope so. But say if you are too busy or tired.
>
> Ivy Compton-Burnett

Of course I was never too busy or tired for Ivy, but I had to change the day to Friday the 17th, two days later.

Her parcel of manuscript lay on the table. There were some new novels lying about and I picked them up and we talked about them. Vita Sackville-West's new novel *No Signposts in the Sea* was one of them. I hadn't read it and Ivy told me to take it with me. 'Read it when you aren't typing,' she said.

I put it on her parcel of manuscript.

'Have you read this?' she asked. It was one of Snow's.

I said he wasn't my author and Ivy said he wasn't hers. I told her a friend of mine who read Henry James and Meredith mostly, even now, loved Snow and bought all his books as soon as they appeared. 'She finds him comforting,' I said.

'Comforting?' Ivy repeated the word. She looked at her parcel of manuscript and our eyes met. Something passed between us, unspoken, 'all of the finest wind-blown intimations' as Henry James would say, and I broke into mirth.

There were no difficulties that day; Ivy was happy and without the usual air of strain about her. And I was always happy when she had written another novel. But she disliked the title. 'Think of a better one for me, will you' she asked, as she saw me to the front door. 'I've called it *The Mighty and their Fall*. I'm not quite satisfied with it, but I can't think of another.'

I promised to do my best.

The novel *The Mighty and their Fall* – certainly a misleading title –

84

has for me all the main ingredients of the best Compton-Burnett. There is the close and obsessive family relationship, this time between father and daughter. In her next novel as in earlier novels, it is between brother and sister, the relationship closest to Ivy's heart. The family of five is a spaced-out one – Egbert, twenty-two, and Lavinia, twenty, then three younger children, Agnes, thirteen, Hengist, eleven, and Leah, ten. Hengist and Leah make the usual shrewd comments most of Ivy's young children make; they are not helpless-seeming, like the children in *Manservant and Maidservant*. Their governess is Miss Starkie, and there is a formidable old grandmother of eighty-seven, Selina Middleton.

In some ways the daughter, Lavinia is a portrait of Ivy herself. She is 'an autocrat and an intellectual' with 'grey eyes . . . fine bones that showed in both her figure and face, and a look of sober humour'.

There is the odd member of the family who is no true relation, the adopted son of Selina's husband which makes him both mysterious and eligible, a device Ivy uses more than once.

Here is a passage where Ivy describes a mishap. The children provide the comedy, and when servants or children are comic Ivy is often at her best. The three younger children are walking out with their governess, watched from the house by Selina.

> Agnes walked in front with Miss Starkie, and Hengist and Leah together behind, indeed arm-in-arm, though this was not their habit. Selina beckoned to her son and returned to her seat. Ninian succeeded her at the window and in a moment leaned out of it.
>
> Something depended from Miss Starkie's skirts, of a nature to unravel when pulled, and her pupils were putting a foot on it in turn, and receding as its length increased.
> 'Miss Starkie, you have suffered a mischance! Some part of your dress is disintegrating. The mischief should be arrested.'
> Miss Starkie turned, paused and stooped, and set off in another direction.
> 'Oh, a bush will serve me, Mr Middleton. I can manage in a moment. Why did you not tell me, children?'
> 'For a reason that is clear,' said Hugo (the uncle), 'Some chances do not come again. Sometimes I regret my childhood. But only for light reasons.'

Another example of Ivy's genius for comedy comes where Selina tells the young children that, after all, their father is not to re-marry.

> She went up to the schoolroom and stood just within it, her eyes fixed almost fiercely upon its occupants.

'Agnes and Hengist and Leah, lend me your ears. I come to bury some-thing, not to praise it. The mistake your father has made will not live after him. I have come to end it with a word. It is a word you will hear in silence, with your eyes fixed on my face. Do not look at each other. Do not utter a syllable or a sound. Your father is not going to be married. He will be a widower, as he has always been. The reasons are not for you to seek. And you will not seek them. Do you hear and understand?'

There was silence.

'Should you not answer your grandmother?' said Miss Starkie, in a rather faint tone.

'She said we were not to speak,' said Leah.

'He can't always have been a widower,' said Hengist. 'No one could begin by being that.'

'As long as you can remember,' said Miss Starkie. 'Always as far as you are concerned.'

The children, undaunted by Grandma's oration, say they will ask their father why he has decided to remain a widower.

'Leah, he will tell you nothing. The subject will not be broached,' (Selina says).

'What does broach mean?' said Leah.

'Leah, it means what you are to know it means. That the subject will not be mooted.'

'Is moot a real word?' said Leah.

In some of the more tragic scenes I heard, as I typed them, Ivy's own voice. When Selina knows she is going to die, she says:

'I don't believe in a future life, or want to. I should not like any form of it I know. I don't want to be a spirit or to return to the earth as someone else. I could never like anyone else enough for that.'

Ivy always said, when asked in interviews, that in childhood she received the usual religious instruction, but had no great liking for it, and ceased to regard religion as in any way necessary or important as soon as she could please herself in the matter. Selina, like Oscar Jekyll, the unbelieving parson in *A House and its Head*, finds the old beliefs convenient with troublesome children.

'They need to accept an all-seeing Eye. Or rather we need them to. No ordinary eye could embrace their purposes. We may as well depute what we can.'

And when the family discuss what is the best thing in life, Ivy's own voice is heard. 'Human friendship?' the son suggests. And Teresa, the second wife, says: 'An affection that would last . . . in ourselves as well as in someone else; that would be a basis for our lives.'

I finished typing the novel by the end of the month, and wrote suggesting a date for bringing it up. Ivy wrote on 3 March 1961.

> I should be grateful if I could have the work by the end of next week as I want to take it away with me. It would be nice if you could come to lunch on Thursday, or Saturday, and bring it.
>
> I. C-B.

I had written earlier to say I had not been able to think of a title. I disliked the one she gave the book and told her that when I read it I thought of the old rhyme about the rain raining every day upon the just and unjust fellow, but more upon the just because the unjust takes the just's umbrella. I quoted the rhyme to her and said the book could be called the Just and the Unjust, but she should give the rhyme on the title page – not at all an 'Ivyish' device, but the only suggestion I could make. Ivy, however, was not against the title but felt she couldn't include the rhyme as well, so we left it.

I had tried to read Vita Sackville-West's last novel in between typing Ivy's book, but found I couldn't get on with it at all. Ivy's strong sentences spoil one for a style as gently poetic as Vita Sackville-West's. I told Ivy I would get it from the library and read it later. 'It's a bit too beautiful alongside your wit and cynicism,' I told her.

Ivy took the book, her eyes amused. 'Yes, it is a bit wishy-washy,' she said.

The Mighty and their Fall came out in September. The reviews were disappointing and somehow misleading. As usual I wrote to Ivy and told her what I thought about them. Her reply is dated 29 September 1961.

> I was so glad to have your letter. I think as you do, and as I believe a good many people must think. Let me know when you come to London, and come and have lunch with me.
>
> Ivy Compton-Burnett

Nearly a year later, in early September 1962, my sister and I moved to a village in the New Forest. Sussex had become rather crowded during the summer, and Hampshire was our county. I wrote telling Ivy of my move and giving her my new address. I also told her that I had written a novel while in Sussex, and then I had pulled it all apart, had tried to rearrange it, but it had gone like Humpty-Dumpty and I couldn't put it together again.

Ivy replied on 5 December 1962.

I was so much interested in your letter. Do put your novel in some sort of form and place it. There is hardly a novel to-day that is a novel at all, and I am tired of being disappointed. I have one on hand, but not yet finished.

What a difficult kind of work to choose! But of course one did not choose it. There was no choice.

Tell me when you come to London, and come and see me. And my best wishes for the book on writers. How pleasant to be too advanced!

The weather here is vile.

Ivy Compton-Burnett

My book on writers had been accepted provisionally by a publisher of schoolbooks, and I had had to change it as it was considered 'too advanced' for schools. I had written it with university students in mind and was finding it difficult to change.

Her remarks on writing being 'a difficult work to choose', is a cry from the heart, and she had said that before. Her technique was severe and demanding. There is nothing loose or slack in her books, and except that she sometimes gives her bores their heads, she holds the reins tight from the first page to the last. Many modern novels she thought loosely put together, and plotless, no novels at all, in fact, in her view. Virginia Woolf wrote well, but, Ivy said, we could not call her a novelist.

I shared her view about the novels of the day, but she reproached me for choosing biographies and non-fiction books rather than novels. I have a letter from her on the subject written the year before she died; I will quote it when I come to that time.

In April 1963 she had finished her new book. Her card is dated 5 April 1963. She writes:

Could you come to luncheon or tea one day to fetch a MS. to type? You will find me in a great muddle. I am turned out of my flat, and have not found another. The scarcity is dreadful of flats above about 2 rooms. I am so glad you are settled.

Ivy Compton-Burnett

This was dire news. Ivy was seventy-seven. She had a weak heart, and I was certain the whole upheaval of moving from a flat that had been her home for almost thirty years would kill her. Her way of life was quiet and ordered; she could stand no other way. And she was defenceless aginst a landlord who gave her notice to quit.

I went up to London as soon as I could. We had to change the date once or twice, and finally I went up on 23 April. Of course I said that I would come after lunch, but she insisted that we have 'a light lunch together' as she had a lot to tell me.

On the way, somewhere between Palace Gate and the turning into Cornwall Gardens, I saw a notice in the porch of a block of new flats, a notice that said there was a penthouse to let, enquire at porter's office. I couldn't see Ivy in a penthouse, but of course there would be a lift, and perhaps a roof garden. I asked the porter, and he told me it was to be let with vacant possession now, unfurnished, at twenty guineas a week. I think it was twenty, it was not less, I know, and may have been more. I said I had no time to see it and would think it over. To my mind such a rent was astronomic. But when I told Ivy about it she wasn't at all shocked. 'Oh, that's what it would be,' she said. 'That's what they are asking now.'

She had almost decided on a flat she had seen in Kensington Square. It was the only flat possible, she said. Others she had seen would not do at all. I asked her why she had to move. She told me her landlord wanted to turn the whole of the first floor over to the Dominican Embassy, that way he would get more money. I knew the only other flat on the first floor was the Dominican Embassy as it was plainly marked.

'He's a Polish landlord,' Ivy said. 'He wants to get as much money as possible for the place.'

We talked about Kensington Square, its quietness and dignity. It was conveniently situated, too, I said, wanting to say soothing things, for hadn't she just finished a novel, strain enough to bear without coping with Polish landlords? I saw she was in a mood, poor Ivy, that might easily ignite. I had never seen her so distressed, and I was distressed for her.

'There are a great many cars standing about,' Ivy said. 'And no one in them.'

It was a time when London squares had become like car parks. I didn't think it a good thing, if Kensington Square was like that, and I said so, as gently as I could.

'Oh, that won't matter,' Ivy said at once. 'If the cars go there to park, they just stop. That isn't noisy.'

89

'No, no, of course not,' I said quickly. I had been thinking of car doors banging day and night, but I didn't say so.

I felt I was on very thin ice during lunch that day, and was pleased when Ivy changed the subject and asked me what I had been doing, and I was able to tell her about an amusing play I had seen – Iris Murdoch's *Severed Head*, perhaps. But I thoughtlessly asked her if she had been to the theatre lately – Ivy was fond of the theatre.

How could she go to plays? she asked me, with this dreadful upheaval hanging over her.

I agreed quickly that of course she couldn't.

Some years later when I talked about this time of crisis to her sister, Vera Compton-Burnett, I said I had felt at the time that Ivy must have a nervous breakdown, it was all more than she could bear. Her sister told me she had had the same fear for her.

We talked of her novel; I told her how much I looked forward to typing it, how lucky I was to have this especial privilege.

'I thought I would have a change this time,' Ivy said, as she handed me the parcel when I was ready to go.

'A change?' I looked at the parcel with alarm, more alarm than I really felt. I knew Ivy couldn't change.

'You'll see,' she told me, a smile in her eyes.

'Oh, now I'm anxious,' I said. 'I wouldn't really like you to change.'

And of course there was no change. It was the mixture as before, two families, neighbours, three generations in one of them, and the butler. But the hero, the 'God' of the title, is a popular author, and this is the change that Ivy referred to. Her hero, heir to a baronetcy, worked for his living.

In an interview in May 1962 she had said: 'I am working very spasmodically. I do not know what is going to happen in it (her novel). It is better to start a book with the main line already prepared, but I cannot always do this. I have to start and hope for the best.'*

What is interesting in this novel is Ivy's implied criticism of writers of 'popular' fiction. Alfred Merton and Hereward Egerton are neighbours and both are writers. The former is a much respected author of academic works, the latter a writer of popular fiction.

'Well, Galleon, and what do you say to my son's manner of life? . . .'

Sir Michael asks his butler.

* Interviewed by W. J. Weatherby. *The Guardian*, 11 May 1962.

'Well, Sir Michael, if there happens to be necessity, it does not involve anything manual,' said Galleon, making this clear.

'Well, I am not so sure. Scratching and scribbling and shuffling papers! It does that into the bargain.'

'Well, not to the point of soiling the hands, Sir Michael.'

This is a servant's criticism of a man in Hereward's position earning his living by writing.

The criticism Hereward receives from his own son Merton is on a different level. Merton is determined to be a writer, but he makes it plain to all the members of the family that he will not follow in his father's footsteps. 'I would rather write nothing than write as he does,' he tells his brothers.

'You would not like to have written my books?' said Hereward . . . .
'Well, to be as honest as you are, Father, I should not.'

Hereward's sister is philosophic. Zillah speaks as Ivy might.

'No writer goes the whole length with any other. Each of them shivers at the lapses of the rest, and is blind to his own. And the youngest shiver the most. And the greatest writers have them.'

There is deep understanding between the brother and sister, Hereward and Zillah. The brother and sister relationship was one of Ivy's main themes, and where she discusses it she always uses the same words. Hereward says:

'Zillah, we are brother and sister. If we were not, what could we be?'
'Nothing that was nearer. It stands first among the relations. There is nothing before it, nothing to follow it. It reaches from the beginning to the end.'

And in *More Women than Men* (1933) Josephine says of a secret between herself and Jonathan, and unknown to Felix, Jonathan's friend:

'He will not want to know. He will leave it between the brother and sister. He knows that that relation goes back to the beginning; that it is the longest, if not the deepest. He will leave it its own silences.'

And in *Elders and Betters*, Mr Donne says:

'The relation of brother and sister goes back to the first days. It has its roots in the beginning. There may be stronger feeling but never the same understanding.'

Hereward, the writer of popular fiction, an author who is, as he says, 'a household word' is the most lecherous of Ivy's men. When he sets eyes on his son's fiancee, he tells her: 'I should have had a daughter. It is what I need . . . It is the classic relation, rooted in the past.'

This misquoting Zillah and one of Ivy's articles of faith makes him seem particularly odious.

I disliked typing the talk of three-year-olds. When the B.B.C. suggested a radio version Ivy insisted on the child's part being kept as it was. This was impossible.

'My last book couldn't be done on the wireless because one of the essential characters was a boy of three. The problem of the voice was really insuperable.' Ivy explained to Anthony Curtis of the *Sunday Telegraph* in 1965.

Her words 'my last book' had another meaning for her, but *A God and his Gifts* was, in fact, her last completed novel.

I finished typing the book early in May, and wrote telling her I would bring it up as I had a date in London. I said I would leave the novel during the morning.

In her note of thanks she added: 'After all, I am staying here, but at great expense!'

This news sent me up to London with a light heart, and the change in her, and in Peggy, her Irish housekeeper – (the one who liked to be spoken to) – was apparent at once.

'I'll bring Miss Greig some sherry, shall I?' Peggy said, all smiles, when she had shown me into the sitting-room.

Ivy said nothing, looking at Peggy. She really disapproved of such forwardness in a maid, but she was having to school herself to what she called 'the new ways'.

'I'll bring the sherry, shall I?' Peggy repeated.

'Thank you, but not for me, Peggy,' I said quickly, as Ivy was still silent. 'I shall be having some before lunch. I mustn't have *too* much, you know.'

Peggy departed, and I talked about my enjoyment of her book.

'And about a *writer* – I enjoyed that.' I told her.

'Yes, well, I thought I would have a change,' Ivy said. She was bright and cheerful. I told her I was delighted to hear she would not have to move after all.

'What made your landlord change his mind?' I asked.

'My having to give references for the Kensington Square flat. I gave them my banker and this landlord. And he came to see me one morning with a letter in his hand. It was from the other landlord asking for his reference. He said: "If you can pay this rent, you can pay me the same, and keep on the flat." '

I was horrified. I said, before I thought, 'Oh well, of course, he's got you on toast.'

There was a pause.

'And you'll stay?' I went on.

'Oh, I'll stay,' Ivy said. 'But don't ask me what the rent will be. As you say, he's got me on toast.'

It was the only time I heard Ivy lapse into schoolgirl jargon. Her eyes were laughing as she said it. Her relief at not having to leave the flat was so obvious that, in spite of my furious feelings against the landlord, I cheered up.

'Well, you'll keep your home,' I said, looking about the familiar room. 'That's wonderful. I'm so glad for you. And of course now you can insist on his giving you a good long lease so that you won't have this upheaval again.'

But she flared up at this, flared and fairly glared at me.

'Oh no . . . no . . . only the working class do that!'

We looked at each other across her small table, Ivy stern and shocked, myself bewildered. But this time I said nothing. This was Ivy talking like Miss Matty of Cranford, and it wasn't for me to tell her that the working class had their rents collected by the rent collector once a week – or those in the poorer quarters do.

'Only the working classes do that,' she repeated, as though I hadn't heard.

But I didn't answer. We let the matter drop and talked of other things. After her death, in August 1969, her housekeeper told me she hoped to be able to stay in the flat until the lease expired in October of that year. So Ivy got her lease after all, and she mentioned it to me later in a letter.

Before I left we spoke of my visit to London as this time I was staying for a few days with a friend. Ivy, as usual, questioned me closely as to my feelings on finding myself in London again. Wasn't I pleased to be back? she asked. And as usual I told her I was thrilled. I said I was so pleased to be in London I wished I was on my own. One had to consider one's hostess; one couldn't just rush out the moment breakfast was over. And that was what I wanted to do. Time was so short, London so vast. I said I wish I could do as a friend of mine did in some relation's house, leave a small case with a nightie and a tooth-brush in a spare room. She came and went periodically, without disturbing anyone. An arrangement that worked very well.

'You can leave a suitcase here,' Ivy said.

This was an amazing thing for Ivy to say and I could hardly believe my ears. I smiled broadly and went on talking to cover my confusion.

'One must of course consider one's hostess,' I said, 'but at the same time one wants to be free . . .'

'You can leave a suitcase here,' Ivy repeated, and she smiled at me encouragingly.

'Thank you very much,' I said. 'That's most kind of you.'

It was time for me to go. I think Ivy was so pleased to be free from the threat of having to move, her veins ran with the milk of human kindness on that day. She was always kind and considerate, and always generous, but I thought such an offer was exceptional. I couldn't quite see myself having the freedom of a spare room in Ivy's flat, in fact to my mind it seemed quite out of the question. I wrote to her some days later thanking her for her kind offer. My plans were always uncertain, I said. I came to London not more than two or three times a year. And now that her rent was so much increased I wouldn't want to add to her electric light bills. On the other hand, if it was possible to arrange something to our mutual advantage, then it would be something we could discuss together when the time came. I know I wrote something like that to her, and then forgot all about it. I really couldn't take her offer seriously, and I think she also thought twice about the matter because in November I had a few lines from her. Her card is dated 10 November 1963.

I find I have to do the whole of my flat up, as it was in the Lease. And the man can come so seldom that I have no idea when it will be finished, probably not for months. So I am so sorry that I can't be depended on. I hope you will find a room you like.

My book comes out on November 21st. Do come and see me soon.

I. C-B.

I was up in London on 11 December for a party and this time I was able to use my sister's bedsitter while she came down to Hampshire. I was in town for three or four days, and had tea with Ivy on one of them. The reviews of *A God and his Gifts* were quite good – Ivy's reviews were always mixed. But I remember on this occasion I was very indignant because the *New Statesman* had allowed Brigid Brophy to review her last novel, and she was quite out of her depth, I considered, in tackling an author like Ivy. Her review really made nonsense of the book, which must have been her aim. But Ivy was philosophic. She knew that that kind of 'smart' writing couldn't hurt her, and on the whole she was quite pleased with the book's reception.

She was far more upset by the state of her flat. The hall was piled with furniture, and remained in that state for months. The painters had started on the dining-room, but worked spasmodically, and Ivy said they never knew from one day to another whether they would come or not. And Peggy, her Irish housekeeper, would have to leave her, perhaps in a month of two, as she was wanted at her home in Ireland. It was a time of unrest for poor Ivy who loved order and quiet. She told me she was living on capital, the cost of everything was very high.

As her chief anxiety was that she might be left without help, when I wrote to her for Christmas I told her to send for me if things became desperate. I quite enjoyed housekeeping, and could cook simple meals. Her reply is dated 7 January 1964.

> Thank you many times. My problem is in abeyance at the moment, but P. has to go back to Ireland before very long. Sufficient unto the day! Do come again soon. With love,
>
> Ivy Compton-Burnett

Fortunately for Ivy, Peggy was able to stay for six months or more. I was up in London in June and stayed this time with Jeanne de Casalis (my sister-in-law by an early marriage). She was at this time suffering from a slow, incurable disease, an anaemia of the brain resulting in almost total loss of memory and premature senility. As her husband was also ill, at this time, and their Italian housekeeper unsympathetic to Jeanne, I went up to help them. My sister and I were devoted to Jeanne and in the years before the war spent some happy holidays with her in her lovely old cottage near Ashford.

Before I returned to Hampshire I telephoned Braemar Mansions and Ivy asked me to come to tea on 23 June. This time I had some news for her. I often stayed at a club in Great Russell Street, and I discovered they needed relief staff during the summer. This time a member of the staff had been ill and had to have an operation. As I knew her and had more than once been in her little office on the second floor, and the job was part-time, I offered to take her place. My offer was accepted at once.

Ivy was pleased. And it pleased her especially that I was pleased to be back in London. Of course such goings-on as picking up jobs in this way left her puzzled, and I assured her it was only part-time and I would have plenty of time for other things.

Neither of us knew that this was the club her sisters, Vera and Julia Compton-Burnett, always used when they came to London for conferences or meetings. I discovered it later when the guest list was sent up to the office, and of course I met them, recognising them instantly as Ivy's sisters. For years both of them had been wholly committed to the Rudolf Steiner philosophy of education. In 1931 they had, jointly, translated his lectures: *Eurythmy as Visible Speech* which had been published in German. When I met them they no longer taught, but were on the Board of Governors. They lived in Hertfordshire.

Ivy told Peggy the news when she saw me to the front door. We had said goodbye to each other, and I was turning to go when Peggy said: 'Oh, wait a second, Miss Greig!' and darted away. I waited and Ivy waited. Peggy was back in a minute.

'For your journey,' she said, thrusting a small packet of chocolate at me. 'Have them for the journey.'

I was taken aback, but thanked her for her kind thought.

'So kind,' I murmured, smiling at Peggy. I stole a look at Ivy. She stood beside me, stiff and grim, without a scrap of expression on her face, her eyes averted from the vulgar scene.

I hoped I nothing common did or mean, thanked Peggy warmly again, said goodbye, and thank-you to Ivy and fled.

On my way home, eating Peggy's chocolate, glad that Ivy couldn't see me, and certain that she herself would be eating a chocolate or two that her friends regularly brought her, I tried to understand Peggy's lapse into kindness from Ivy's point of view. It was embarrassing to receive presents from 'those in service', and it was wrong to cause embarrassment, and Peggy should know her place. Was that it? I remembered when Margaret Jourdain was alive the maid, one of the silent kind, always made small cream cheeses in summer from sour milk. Ivy and I used to eat it with our cucumber and lettuce for tea. And sometimes, when Ivy saw me to the front door, she would point to a small parcel on the hall table and say: 'I see she's left you one of those little cheeses.' And she would be quite pleased, and hand me the little parcel, and of course I would take it gratefully and thank Ivy very much and say how kind. 'She' was never thanked, at least not by me: she was invisible.

The difference between the gift of the cheese from the nameless 'she', and Peggy's offering of chocolate was a subtle one. And soon after I received a note of apology. It was dated 24 June 1964. Ivy wrote:

> You must forgive Peggy for making you a gift. It is one of her Irish eccentricities and there have been other victims. It was so nice to see you. Do come again soon.
>
> Ivy Compton-Burnett

I wrote briefly in return thanking her for my pleasant afternoon. I said I knew the Irish were generous and impulsive, and of course one wouldn't dream of repulsing such a generous gesture. I told Ivy I hoped to be able to see her more often now that I would be in London regularly.

I didn't see Peggy again.

4

The year 1965 was a sad year for Ivy and for her friends. It marked a turning point in these last years of her life. In April she was ill, and I have a letter from her dated 22 April 1965.

Dear Miss Greig,

It is always so nice to hear from you, but this time my response is poor.

My novel is still in an early stage, and I am myself disabled by a mild heart trouble and have to be slow.

My housekeeper left 3 weeks ago, but she is replaced by an elderly 'companion', who does most things and is nice.

There seem no good novels, and I am placed as you are.

I *do* hope you will come to see me a little later when I am well and you have more time.

For the moment this is all I can do. And not much.

Yours ever,

Ivy Compton-Burnett

I am not really ill, but of course there is Anno Domini!!

I was certain this trouble was brought about by all the worry and upheaval of the previous year. She was very sensible about her health, however, and I knew she would recognise the danger signals and take care.

In May I wrote to congratulate her on the success of *A Heritage and its History*, the play Julian Mitchell had made of the novel. It was shown first at the Oxford Playhouse, and then in May at the Phoenix Theatre, London. The reviews I saw were all good, and critics talked about her 'delicious wit' – 'witty as the highest of high comedies' – and the plays 'intellectuality, so sure of itself that it is without self-consciousness.' (I quote from Philip Hope-Wallace and Harold Hobson.)

Ivy replied, her letter dated 25 May 1965, and used my Christian name for the first time. She wrote:

Let us use each other's Christian names.

I have not seen the play, as I can't do stairs at the time, and they are

98

everywhere. And in a way I shrank from seeing it! I felt that a book should be left as it was written.

The notices are good, though they vary, of course and I hope it will hold its way for a while. Though the *Evening Standard* gave it a fortnight! And some insults!

I have been in domestic trouble. Peggy had to go as her family were returning to Ireland. Then a working companion who wd. have done, had the offer of a charity flat to retire in, and will have to go after about 2 months. An elderly working woman, a widow with a married family is supposed to replace her, and I hope for the best! I have not been *left*, but Life is not easy in this welfare state.

I am well in myself now, but still have the weak leg muscles. I hope you are both well, and able to do your own domestic work. Dependence has increasing problems, and I am dependent.

Thank you so much for your letter.

Yours as ever,
Ivy Compton-Burnett.

When I wrote I told Ivy that her letter, the first sentence, had made me very happy. So many of her notes to me were on cards that I was hardly aware of her not using my Christian name – we used no names in conversation. I always signed myself by my Christian name, but of course it was not for me to suggest we call each other Ivy and Cicely. Ivy was a generation older and belonged to the age when even engaged couples were slow to adopt Christian names. The rest of her letter was sad. Poor Ivy was to have staff troubles for several months longer.

In June my sister and I were up in London to see the play. We enjoyed it tremendously, and I thought it came over well, on the whole. The first impact, so startling when read, was blurred on the stage. Visually it was good, the dinner table and Deakin the butler, and the members of the family made a delightful scene. But the usual throwaway lines a dramatist uses while the audience is still fidgetting and trying to tune in to the different voices were not there to help us. Ivy doesn't begin her books with throwaway lines. However, once we were tuned in it was undoubtedly the language, the Ivy sentences, that held us in thrall. The music of such a sentence as Julia's – one I have quoted before:

'. . . It may be to say that I am a woman and a mother, but what is there against my being both? And what is there to prevent it? And why should I be any better if I were neither?'

came over most movingly and beautifully.

I wrote a full account of our afternoon to Ivy, and said I felt sure, barring a crisis or something, it would have a run. I thought Deakin was not quite her Deakin, he leaned against the sideboard too often, and tended to look bored while the family ate and talked. He was more like a hotel waiter than a family butler, with ears pricked for news to take to the servants' hall.

Ivy wrote back on 14 June.

> Thank you so much for telling me about the play. I have not been able to go owing to stairs, and a cough and domestic changes. The 'companion' has had to go, as she was offered a free flat. Nice but too grand. And I have just got one elderly, working-class widow, who seems to promise well.
>
> Forgive scrawl. The play has led to a great deal of correspondence. I will indeed bear in mind your offer of help in dire need!
>
> As always,
> Ivy

This was the first time Ivy had apologised for her scrawl. And it was really not as wild on this note as on others I have had from her. She was a natural scrawler with her correspondence, and a very neat writer with her novels, written in pencil. It is one of the remarkable things about her.

A 'companion' – the word always in inverted commas – would not have done at all for Ivy, and it was a pity the Agency sent them to her. She knew too much about servants ever to get used to the idea that anyone 'in service' could ever be a companion. I remember one day her telling us that the under-servants in her home were called 'squalors'. Before her day the poor things were of the rough peasant class and often beaten. Swift beat his servant Patrick; I remember being shocked when I read of his rages with Patrick in his *Journal to Stella*. Later servants had a better standing in the home, loyalty was mutual, and help, too, was mutual. And 'servants were such fun', as Ivy said in an interview.

I was not in London again that year. I had the chance of a two months' visit to France in September, a month in Etretat and a month in Paris, and I went. I have always loved Paris and have got to know it pretty well by walking as much as possible. I sent Ivy a postcard telling her I was in heaven.

In November I was home again and in December I wrote to her as usual for Christmas. Ivy's answer, a postcard, dated 21 December 1965, was a shock. Her own address was crossed out, and in a thin, rather careful scrawl she had written her present address:

> Private Wing,
> University College Hospital
> Gower St. W.1.
>
> I am here with a broken hip. A sad misfortune! Thank you for your letter.
>   Every good wish and love,
>
>   Ivy C-B.

Later she told me that the news had been in the papers. I had seen nothing. And her card had suffered the usual Christmas delay so that it was too near Christmas when I got it for me to go to London. I wrote at once telling her I hoped to see her after Christmas: it was difficult to say what I felt beyond the usual hope that she was not in too much pain. I tried to imagine Ivy in hospital. She could cope with surgeons and doctors, but not, I felt, with all the nursing drill, the washing and being tidied up and changed, and all the brisk jollying of the nurses. Would they tell her to be a good girl, now, and eat up her dinner?

After Christmas I slipped on some ice and ricked my back, and was quite useless for several days. On 13 January I was able to go to the club in Great Russell Street, but when I telephoned the hospital I was told that Miss Compton-Burnett had returned the day before. Ivy's housekeeper, one unknown to me, told me that Ivy enjoyed visits and would like to see me. She had to go to bed at five because of the day nurse going off, so would I come not later than four.

The flower shops in Kensington were full of early spring flowers. I chose snowdrops and violets and polyanthus, two or three bunches of each, for Ivy. The door was opened by a large fair woman, a new housekeeper, who greeted me with the words: 'She's waiting for you!'

When I opened the sitting-room door I saw Ivy in her usual chair. There were crutches on the sofa, and a folded blanket. She turned to greet me and when I saw her face I realised at once how differently people react to pain and surgery and hospital. I had often visited friends who had had the same accident as Ivy, and thought that they had looked quite pleased with life, on the whole, and I put it down to the spoiling and visits and flowers and fuss – a break from the usual, perhaps monotonous round. But Ivy was different. Her face was gaunt, haggard, and had a ravaged look. The neat, strong features were puffy, her cheeks sunken, her skin colourless. Even her hair, always so tidily folded away, had an abandoned look. Her dignity, the 'iron dignity' critics wrote about, had suffered outrage. I nearly wept at sight of her.

She said 'Hullo, Cicely!' in her quiet way. When we had greeted each other she asked to see the flowers. I sat beside her and showed her the different ones, and as always, and with her usual lovely courtesy, she showed pleasure, touching the small bunches one by one, and smelling the violets. There were other flowers in the room, azaleas and a bowl of beautiful cyclamen.

I said I hoped there had not been much pain. Ivy said no, not much really. More discomfort than pain.

'And the being rolled about in bed by nurses. Why do they roll us about?'

We talked about that as I had had a spell in hospital, and we compared our different experiences. But we had both been 'rolled about'. And now, she said, looking about the room, it was wonderful to be home again.

There was no pain, she went on, but everything that one was meant to sit on was much too low. The chairs, and the lavatory, and the edge of the bed. One sat down and one couldn't get up again. One had to have help. There were two nurses, one for day and one for night. It would be a slow business. The surgeon had told her it must be twelve weeks at least before he could say for certain that her hip was mended. Six weeks had passed since the operation. And he had gone abroad.

'He neglects his patients,' she told me. 'He's somewhere in Austria.'

At the end of twelve weeks there would be another X-ray. Meanwhile she tried always never to jar her hip. But it jarred so easily.

'Where was it you fell?' I asked.

'Here, in this room where I've lived for over thirty years,' she told me, sounding rather like Selina in *The Mighty and their Fall* might have sounded.

'I caught my foot in that rug which has been there for over thirty years. I seemed to run forward, and I couldn't stop myself, and then I fell and I thought I had died. Then I found I hadn't died, but I could not get up. The supper bell went, and I didn't move. After a quarter of an hour she came to look for me, and found me on the floor. She's big and strong and was able to lift me on to a chair. The chair had castors, so she was able to wheel me into the bedroom. Then she rang for the doctor, and fortunately he was at home. I was X-rayed that evening. Men had to come from Chiswick.'

This was how Ivy gave me the details of her accident. She had that way of speaking that makes one remember her sentences. It is the Ivy rhythm.

I said I hoped the press hadn't got to hear of it, and that photographers wouldn't try to take her with her crutches.

But the press had got to know, and indeed she was glad of it. It let people know where she was, and why the flat was empty so often. I told her I had been in France during October. I had seen nothing in the *Guardian* in November.

'It was in the *Guardian*,' Ivy said. 'Everyone was very kind. There were flowers and grapes every day. I had to send some of the grapes down to the kitchen, there were so many. *The Times* and the *Telegraph* had the news in. My sisters were so good about coming to see me, oh, they *were* so good!'

I said I wished I had come.

'You might break me off three grapes,' she said.

I carefully broke three grapes from a bunch of beautiful, black grapes.

Her housekeeper had made tea for her, and had cut me a slice of what Ivy called 'very stale cake'.

She urged me to put jam on it. Without jam it would be quite uneatable, she said.

I did as I was told, though really I was not hungry. And I had my eye on the clock.

'Your housekeeper told me you went to bed at five,' I said.

Ivy said there was plenty of time.

She had so often told us that there was a great part of present-day life she knew nothing about; and I reminded her of this, and asked her if she had found this new experience, looked at objectively, and in retrospect, at all interesting.

'I mean interesting enough to write about,' I said.

Of course I knew what her answer would be, but I hoped for some comment on the human predicament as she found it in hospital.

She agreed it was a different life, but it was one she would not want to write about. And she had gone to a private ward. She had felt she couldn't stand a public ward, and I agreed I didn't think she could.

Before I went she asked me what books I had read. She had not been able to read in hospital.

'When I fell I had been reading Iris Murdoch's new novel *The Green and the Red*. Of course it was returned to the library when I went to hospital. And in hospital I couldn't read. I just looked at newspapers and magazines. I couldn't read a book.'

I had read Iris Murdoch's novel and not cared for it much. I didn't like books about the Irish troubles.

'I don't feel inclined to finish it,' Ivy said. 'There's too much in it about religion, and I dislike books about religion.'

I said goodbye to her.

'Will you tell the nurse that I'm ready. The day nurse has to get me settled before the night nurse comes. The expense is terrible. But a night nurse is necessary. It's difficult for me alone not to jar my leg. And when I do jar it, it's painful.'

I promised to tell her. We said goodbye again, and I left Ivy with the nurse.

I was up in London in March when a friend of mine had a show of his paintings. I had picked as many flowers as I could at that time of the year for Ivy, a real garden bunch, and I went to Braemar Mansions straight from Waterloo. The door was answered by the day nurse who assured me that Ivy would be pleased to see me as there was no one with her. She went ahead to announce me and Ivy looked up with her quick smile.

She looked better, but older. The ordeal of all she had been through, and the worry of the expense, and the fear of those jarring pains had left her with a look of weary anxiety. She was pleased with my garden bunch and examined the different flowers.

'What's that one?' she asked.

It was a beautiful spray of Hellebore Foetidus.

'It's one of the Hellebores, Ivy. It looks pretty but it doesn't smell very nice. We have a big clump of it.'

I didn't tell her it was called stinking hellebore, and of course I knew she was a Latin scholar so I said: 'It's not a strong smell. Only when you hold it to your nose. It won't smell in the room.'

But the Mahonia had a very sweet smell and she liked it especially. She asked me to write down the names of the flowers she didn't know. We talked of the Latin names for flowers, the international names, and the local names, like Grannie's Bonnet for Acquilegia. When I had put the flowers in water I told her how much better she was looking. Ivy said she hoped the surgeon would give her a good report.

'I hope he will tell me the bone has knitted all right,' she said. 'It's such a slow business.'

I agreed it was a slow business. I had once broken an arm and I was in plaster for weeks.

'How old were you then?' Ivy asked, with quick interest.

'Oh, about twenty-three.'

'Ah! So even with young people it takes a long time.'

She looked relieved.

'I fell off my horse,' I told her, mentioning this simply to take her mind off her own troubles. I didn't for a moment think she would find this item of my life's story interesting. But as it happened I had made a lucky opening. Her eyes lit up with interest.

'You fell off your horse? Did you ride side-saddle?'

I told her I had never ridden side-saddle, always astride.

'And you fell off.' It was a statement, and it told me that she had ridden side-saddle.

'Perhaps if I'd ridden side-saddle I wouldn't have fallen off. I rode with my brother. Perhaps I wanted to ride like him . . .'

We discussed it. She told me she used to ride with her brothers on the Downs behind Hove.

'Lovely places for riding,' I agreed. I told her I had learned to ride on the beach.

'Oh, the horses like that,' Ivy said.

'Even walking was lovely,' she said, with a sort of mild ecstasy.

'Oh yes, bliss,' I agreed. 'Ambling along on an old horse, hedge-high . . .'

For a few minutes we were away with our memories, with our brothers, and our horses. She asked me if I rode in London. I said no, never. For one thing I couldn't afford to. And I didn't think it much fun trotting round in the Row.

'Well, but they gallop,' Ivy said.

For once I contradicted her. 'They canter,' I said. 'I don't think they would dare do more with all those nursemaids and poodles about.'

I didn't really know, of course, but it amused her. It was a subject we could talk about endlessly, and it took her mind off her troubles. I wondered why the men and women in her novels did not ride. They all have their carriages and traps and stables but none of her heroes that I can remember ride about the countryside as Jane Austen's heroes do.

E   105

I wanted to ask her, but decided I wouldn't. I asked instead if she had been able to take up her writing again.

She said no, she couldn't write. 'This is a misfortune,' she told me, as though trying to make me understand. 'And there is no silver lining to it. No silver lining. And the expense is dreadful. The surgeon is coming tomorrow. I haven't had his bill yet. Well, it must all come out of capital.'

Another worry was the problem of the night nurse.

'I don't really need a night nurse now, but I don't like to tell her so. How can I tell a night nurse I don't need her any more?'

I said I thought her doctor could deal with that. 'Doctors arrange for us to have nurses,' I said. 'Now he can tell the nurse he thinks you will be all right on your own. Nurses take their orders from doctors without question.'

But Ivy was not an easy person to advise. This was all a new experience for her, and she shook her head doubtfully.

'I don't think he would do it,' she said. 'I don't think it would be any use my asking him.'

So I left the subject, but I wrote to the doctor and told him how troubled she was. I don't know what he did about it because I wasn't able to get to London again till September. In May I skidded on a greasy floor and put my knee-cap out. When the surgeon had put it back I had to wear a plaster splint and attend physiotherapy three times a week, and hospital clinics. I was limping about or being taken to and fro in hospital cars for most of the summer. I wrote to Ivy explaining why I hadn't been to see her; I hoped to be at the club early in September. As usual, I told her what books I had read. Violette Leduc's *La Bâtarde* was one that I enjoyed, especially the first part. This was the part that dealt with the author's experiences as a Lesbian. It was the first time I had read such a frank account, though I had read *The Well of Loneliness* and Lady Troubridge's book on her life with Radcliffe Hall. Neither of them were as startling as the French book. I didn't think Ivy would be especially interested in the French goings-on with the ancient sin of Sodomy – it was crude compared to Ivy's subtler suggestion of it in such a book as *More Women than Men*.

Ivy wrote on 12 July 1966.

> Sad news about your knee. You must take care not to strain it.
> I am said to be doing very well, and have given up nurses, and I am

glad to say, the expense of them, but don't yet do steps, or go out, except on the balconies.

I have not read La Batarde, but may do so.

Come to see me when you can. I am well in myself. And forgive this scrawl from a chair.

With love,
Ivy.

When I went to town in early September I was just in time to go to the usual fortnightly R.H.S. Flower Show in Vincent Square. It was the second day, an hour before the show ended. We were allowed to buy, as usual, any flowers or flower arrangement we liked, and I decided to buy an arrangement for Ivy and pay her a surprise visit. The one I chose was a charming and simple arrangement of pinks, mauve and white mixed with Senecio.

I hoped she would be at home, but was dismayed to see a small parcel someone had left on the doormat. I rang the bell and hoped for the best.

There was a silence. After a moment I peered cautiously through the letterbox and saw a light in the hall. I rang the bell again. It seemed a pity to leave the flowers on the doormat. This time I heard Ivy's voice.

'All right! All right! Please wait a minute. I'm coming.'

And I heard the thump, thump, of her aluminium supports – they were not really crutches – as she came along. I felt every shade of shame and confusion it was possible to feel. I held the flowers in front of me like a shield. Then Ivy did something to the handle of the front door and called out: 'Now if you would push the door gently please.'

The door was heavy and rather stiff. I pushed carefully and Ivy gave a cry of alarm. 'Oh, gently please, or you'll knock me over.'

I froze with terror. Then I put my mouth to the letter box and asked if she would stand to one side. I said that anyway I would push as gently as possible. It isn't an easy matter to push a heavy door gently, but I managed to squeeze myself in by inches, and, face to face with Ivy, apologised for having brought her to the door.

She stared at me in silence, but her stare was pleasant. I had been recently to the hairdresser – a detail Ivy noticed always – and instead of a hat I had on one of those small caps made entirely of net and a few bright beads. I had seen them in Paris during the summer. In 1965 women in Paris were hatless, but they wore these little net caps to keep their hair neat. Ivy was clearly greatly taken with my net; she could always express her thoughts very clearly without saying a word, and

I've had the most withering glances hurled at me. Her silence could be ruthlessly disapproving but she never spoke rudely. Now her silence was pleasant, she looked well, and she looked cheerfully glad to see me.

'I thought you were the chemist,' she said, when we had greeted each other.

'Yes, I am the chemist,' I said, holding up the parcel from the doormat.

By now she had forgotten the chemist and the hairnet and was examining the flowers. I told her how I had come by them. They were a great success. It was her housekeeper's day off, and I said I would put them in a bowl. We went into the kitchen.

'There are vases there,' Ivy said, pointing to four horrible glass chimneys.

I asked for a bowl.

'Oh, you'll find bowls in there,' Ivy said, pointing to a cupboard.

I put the flowers in the sink and searched the cupboard. It was full of provisions – rice, jam, flour and things like that.

'I can't see any bowls,' I said. 'This is where she keeps her provisions.'

'There's a bowl there,' Ivy said, pointing to a large mixing bowl.

'Oh, I mustn't use that,' I said. 'It's a mixing bowl. She uses it for cakes and pastry and puddings.'

'Well, but it's a bowl,' Ivy said, with her cold logic.

'Yes, but much too big for pinks. Never mind, They can stay in it until your housekeeper comes back. I'll put water in it.'

When I had put the flowers in the huge bowl, Ivy looked at them. Of course they looked ridiculous, but I said nothing.

'This one is too big,' Ivy said. 'There's a green bowl in my bedroom.'

I looked round her bedroom, a bleak, functional sort of place, with solid, useful furniture, just like a man's bedroom. The bowl was papier-maché and really meant for fruit. I doubted if it would hold water, but by this time I was getting bored with this hunt for a bowl and decided it would have to do.

We went into the sitting-room. Ivy asked me if I knew the name of those particular pinks. I did; they were called 'Grannie's Favourites', so of course I said I didn't know.

'That grey leaf is Senecio,' I said. 'If you stick it in one of your balcony boxes it will grow. It grows very easily from cuttings.'

We sat down before the usual box of chocolates. The room was darkened, the blinds all pulled half-way down. Ivy said: 'I was half-expecting my friend Herman Schrijver. I have to draw the blinds because he finds the light trying to his eyes.'

She had spoken to me before of Herman Schrijver and I knew he was one of her greatest friends. Charles Burkhardt dedicated his book on Ivy to him, and acknowledges the help he gave him in his preface.

I said I wouldn't stay long, but she must tell me how the second book Julian Mitchell had dramatised was going. This was *A Family and a Fortune* which had come over very well on the radio. Julian Mitchell's play from the book had opened in Manchester to good notices. Then it ran for two weeks in Golders Green as no West End theatre was available. There was a very good cast and as there seemed to be no theatre for it they were not able to wait. And Julian Mitchell had told her he wouldn't turn any more of her books into plays; he hadn't realised, he said, how much of the book is lost when it is turned into a play. Of course we both agreed with that. Ivy has never quite liked the idea of her books being re-made as plays when she had used a technique which made them half plays and half novels. That was how she liked them to be thought of, and as they were they came over very well on the wireless, but as Julian Mitchell had said, much of the book was lost as a stage production.

'He's gone to live in the country,' Ivy went on. 'And now he has a chance of writing film scripts. But he says that's really a dreadful come-down.'

At that time I had only read one of his novels. It was about the colour question, a subject I was tired of at the time, so I left it.

'Yes, that's the worst of writers today,' Ivy said. 'They will write about something. Instead of just writing about people, about their characters.'

I said perhaps they felt committed, and used their pen as a weapon because it was mightier than the sword. It was an eighteenth century way of writing, and I liked the eighteenth century.

'Today is very different,' Ivy said. 'There is nothing one would want to write about in the scene today. Oh, nothing!'

How she dismissed our scene, the only scene we knew and, strangely, the scene she knew nothing about. But she was full of good humour that day, and much better. I asked her what news of the housekeeper. The last one, she said, had asked her for more money.

'I pay £6 a week. But she wanted £8 which I wouldn't go to. So she left. But someone who came when she was on holiday, and suited me very well, has come. I was able to get her. She isn't so grand. I don't like them too grand. This one is more of a maid, and that's an advantage because it means she's been trained by upper-class people. I call her Mary and she calls me Madam. I like that.'

Mary Maguire stayed with Ivy till she died. She was a simple, willing and friendly Irish woman. Soon she knew all Ivy's friends, and they all knew her, and she quickly accepted the strange régime, the long teas, and the visitors and the many telephone calls, as a new way of life.

'Now I can't go out, you see,' Ivy said, as we said goodbye. 'So you must come and see me.'

But as I was in town for not much more than a week I returned home without seeing Ivy again, and it was not until the following March 1967, the club once more short-handed, I was in London again. I had written to Ivy from the country telling her I was coming and I would telephone when I arrived. I remember I wrote almost gaily, I said by now I supposed she was walking about normally, and gardening as of old.

The first names I noticed on the guest list were Miss V. Compton-Burnett, and Miss J. Compton-Burnett, Ivy's two sisters, Vera and Julia, the former a larger edition of Ivy, with the same features and alert rather strict look.

'How is Ivy?' I asked them. 'I haven't seen her since September'.

They told me Ivy had fallen and broken the other hip. She had been in hospital for six weeks, and was now home again. And of course there were two nurses, as before.

'But she's very well,' they assured me. 'And quite cheerful.'

Because my first note to Ivy must have sounded rather callous I sent another note round to Braemar Mansions telling her I had just heard the news from her sisters, and I still hoped to see her. The next morning, crossing my note, there was a card from her.

> Did you know I had broken the *other* hip, and been in hospital again for six weeks, and put back further than ever?
>
> I am at home again now, though with nurses, and should like so much to see you at almost any time.
>
> With love,
Ivy.

When I telephoned Mary told me she had had no visitors that day, and I could come any time. I said I couldn't be there before five.

I took wallflowers because they were sweet-smelling, and daffodils. Mary showed me into Ivy's bedroom, and there was poor Ivy in bed, but not looking nearly so ill as when she had come from hospital before.

After her usual careful examination of my flowers she said:

'So you saw my sisters?'

It was the first time she had heard of their using the same club. 'Do they *sleep* there?' she asked.

I told her they had come to town for a conference. Ivy listened with a puzzled air. Her sisters belonged to the professional and working world, their various pursuits and activities a mystery to Ivy. She gave it up.

'Tell me what you've been doing,' she said.

To please her I said: 'Well, I'm enjoying being in London again.'

She asked what I enjoyed especially.

'Being anonymous,' I said at once. 'In our village one can't be that. The moment I walk out of my gate I greet someone or I'm greeted, and that goes on all the way to the village shop. I don't have to say good-morning to a soul in London outside the club. No one knows me. It's marvellous.'

'You might greet one or two people, perhaps, during a day in London,' Ivy said. 'But in the village the first person you said good-morning to would tell the person she was with that Miss Greig had new boots on, and then they would go on to discuss your new boots between themselves, and say that they thought them not quite suitable.'

For the next few minutes we 'acted' like a pair of village gossips almost hilariously. Ivy was in fine form. And how typical that she said 'boots'! How long since women wore boots? And I swear she didn't mean the fashionable long boots teenagers had just begun to wear at that time. Ivy would not have known about them.

'Tell me about yourself,' I said, when we had finished our joking. 'I didn't even know you had had a second fall. I seem always to miss news of sensational happenings.'

She told me she had fallen backwards when she was in the bathroom.

'When I fell first I fell backwards. Now I've broken the other hip. And I got bronchitis in hospital.'

At eighty-two it was really a miracle that she was alive at all, I thought. She was wonderfully brave, amazingly resilient. The discomfort and expense, the nurses and the prolonged lameness must have discouraged and depressed her, but she seemed much less shocked and unhappy after this second fall. And she was fortunate in her friends, most of whom lived near enough to be able to see her often.

I was in London for three weeks altogether and fixed a time with the nurse to see her again. 'You're to come to tea on Monday at 4 o'clock,' I was told.

'How is she?' I asked.

'Oh, much better. You'll see a difference.'

I was shown into the dining-room when I arrived, delayed by a traffic jam in Oxford Street. Ivy was sitting in her usual place, her walking aid by her side. She was sitting lower in her chair now and looked smaller. And she was to look smaller, or so I thought, every time I saw her until she died.

There were three others beside myself, one, a Mrs Sidgewick, I had met when Margaret Jourdain was alive. She had a magnificent collection of Chinese porcelain. She died a year before Ivy and left her collection, the Sidgewick Bequest, to the British Museum. The others were two great friends of Ivy's, Dr Furlong and Mr Pritchett. Both looked after her garden for her, more and more as she got feebler, watering it, sowing seeds, so that it always looked gay. And from window-boxes full of window-box plants – petunias and wallflowers, as in Margaret Jourdain's day, they had become small herbaceous borders with hydrangea and pinks, thrift and roses and snapdragons – all the usual bedding plants, and with heathers and primroses and polyanthus and the usual bulbs in spring. The fuschias were there too, one of Ivy's favourites, and pretty variegated ivies.

On this afternoon we talked about the books we had all been reading, especially those on the Millais–Effie–Ruskin circle. Ivy had enjoyed the letters.

'No one writes letters today,' she said. 'Rose Macaulay's to her sister should never have been published. They were about trivial things, arranging a place to meet, and so on. Too many letters that told us nothing.'

Mrs Sidgewick had been to the exhibition of Pre-Raphaelite paintings.

'How badly Millais painted,' she said, almost indignantly. 'If only he had painted Ophelia *under* the water. . . .'

We had been reading Bertrand Russell's first volume of letters and autobiography which led to talk about Logan Pearsall Smith (whom I disliked), and I can't think by what line to a new book on Keats and Severn, and to mention of a contemporary woman writer whose writings I had always admired and enjoyed. Ivy had known her years ago.

'Margaret and I used to see a lot of her,' she said. 'But success spoiled her. She got impossible. We gave up seeing her. She's become a mixture of the Blessed Virgin Mary and Queen Elizabeth.'

Mostly Ivy said very little at these gatherings; she preferred to listen (as I did . . .), and she listened with keen attention and enjoyment. The teapot now was too heavy for her and Dr Furlong usually poured out, or Elizabeth Sprigge.

I was home again in April and in June I read the news that she had been made a Dame of the British Empire in the Birthday Honours. I wrote congratulating her and told her I hoped to see her in July. Her card in return was dated 12 June 1967.

> Thank you so much.
> Do come when you can in July, at 4 if it is convenient for you.
> I am still doing well, but it is early days yet after the second fall.
>
> > With love,
> > Ivy.

From this time, until her death, Ivy was, by her own will, a prisoner in her flat. When, during a visit in May 1968, I asked her if she had gone out at all, I wished at once I had not asked her. She was gently shocked by my question: 'Oh *no* . . . no . . .' she said, 'I don't go out.'

'You've got your lovely balcony, your garden,' I said, quickly.

'I garden every day,' she told me. 'I like to do the deadheading myself, then I get to know the flowers. A kind friend does the watering for me.'

She had no longing to go out. Her world had always been a small one, and the new strange world of the sixties with its strong accent on youth – 'as in the days of Henry VIII,' Ivy once told us – this was not her world. Her friends came to her, and were pleased to come to her as she was pleased to have them. But now she could write only fitfully. One asked if she was writing, and her answer was always the same.

'I haven't much time for it. I do a little when I have. My post is a heavy one. Someone helps me sometimes with letters. They send some-one from the agency.'

Her misfortunes, however, had one silver lining. They had limited her movements so that she no longer went out, and she hardly wrote at all after 1965. But her doctor told me after she died that really her life was prolonged by her quieter life; she had had a bad heart for years: this was the rest it needed.

Meanwhile I visited her whenever I came to London and I wrote telling her about any interesting books I had read when I was at home. We had, in the three years or so before her death, quite a feast of letters, biographies and autobiographies. Early in 1968 I read the Diaries and Letters of Harold Nicolson. In the second volume he describes a dinner he attended at Trinity College, Cambridge. An elderly butler, one of the old school of butlers, and from his description a thoroughly 'Ivyish' butler, served at his table. Nicolson was impressed by the silver and the formality, and commented on the old traditions to the butler, who replied: 'Civilisation is always recognisable, sir,' a remark Bullivant might have made. I wrote telling Ivy about it, and about Michael Holroyd's book on Lytton Strachey and others. Her answer held a veiled reproach.

> 5, Braemar Mansions,
> S.W.7.
> Jan: 25, 1968.

Dear Cicely,

Yes, I read Harold's two books with great pleasure. Also Angus Wilson's, when I realised it was essentially a book of short stories. An organic whole it is not, and why so long?

Talking of butlers, they repeated 'Manservant and Maidservant' on the wireless some weeks ago, and I liked to renew my friendship with my servant's world. I had to use some strategy to prevent Mary, my house-keeper, from hearing it, as I felt the world was getting *old*-world indeed. I am getting Iris Murdoch's book as a present, and shall wait for it to come.

I think most people chiefly read diaries and biographies nowadays. A novel is more difficult to read, as its parts are related, and don't just go straight on, and it does not provide tit-bits; and it is so often not worth the effort.

Julian Mitchell has brought me a copy of his novel, to come out in a few weeks' time, but I have barely begun it.

I am beginning to walk feebly, but to *walk*, and am held to be doing well.

Considering my age, my frail bones and lack of muscle I wondered I had survived, and I suppose the surgeon did too.

I am getting back into a little book I began some time ago, but a day is so short and interrupted. Don't you find it so?

I wish you lived in London. Distant domiciles mean a virtual separation. But come if and when you can.

With love,
Ivy.

Angus Wilson had never been quite one of her favourite authors – as Anthony Powell and L. P. Hartley were, to name only two. I had the impression that Ivy had never been quite one of his favourites, either, from his article written in the *Observer* after her death – 31 August 1969. He wrote:

Some things, I am sure, she did not do because she could not – she had, for example, no ear for sentence structure or for the euphony of words.

He paid generous tributes to other gifts of hers. But to say this about her sentences suggests he thought her no writer at all: A story-teller who could make us laugh – 'laugh subtly, laugh a great deal'; she had wit and 'extraordinary wisdom'. And 'no ear for sentence structure'. Amazing!

'The little book' as she always spoke of her last novel, was begun in the winter of 1964–5 and laid aside until this year. Now she was 'getting back' into the writing of it.

I was in London in the spring. As I turned into Cornwall Gardens I marvelled how little this corner of London had changed in over twenty years. The houses had grown shabbier, the window boxes gayer, and one or two gardens, re-planted, had become more interesting. Ivy had asked me to come at four.

Mary opened the door, and greeted me.

'Dame is very well,' she told me.

But Ivy had lost two of her friends since I last met her, one of them Mrs Sidgewick, who collected Chinese porcelain.

'She died of a surfeit of lemons,' Ivy informed us at tea. 'Her doctor says she had taken about twenty a day, and the lining of her stomach was corroded away.'

The other friend had died 'of hatreds'. 'She hated everyone and everything. She didn't hate me,' Ivy said.

Both friends were of her generation, and had known Margaret.

Without being too gloomy we talked of recent deaths, and it led to the question of heart transplants, a subject very much in the news at that time. Ivy was emphatic in her disapproval. All transplants were wrong, whatever the organ. But most of all heart transplants were abhorrent to her.

'When I read of one having been done I always hope the person will die. And they do die, don't they? Out of thirteen only three have survived to date.'

This was said quite gently, and altogether sincerely. The whole idea of heart transplants horrified her.

The other guests had to leave early for an evening engagement. Ivy asked me to stay on for a little. We went out to the balcony and I watered while Ivy picked off some dead flowers. But it was windy. England was becoming a windier place, Ivy informed me. She always disliked Brighton because it was so windy. We went in, out of the wind.

One of her books, *A Family and a Fortune*, had been arranged for television by Julian Mitchell. Ivy had bought a set for Mary but had never watched herself. However she and Julian Mitchell and Mary had all watched the play together, an experience much enjoyed by Ivy. She had hoped Mary had enjoyed it too.

'I asked her the next morning if she felt tired after sitting up to watch the play,' Ivy said. 'And Mary said, "Yes, it was very fatiguing".'

This pleased Ivy enormously. And she knew I liked to hear 'real-life' examples of servants' talk as she had written it in her novels. I had always defended her against the charge of exaggeration. Old servants, having heard the talk of their superiors for most of their lives – and this was true of Mary – set an example to those beneath them by talking 'above their station', lifting their vocabulary too high, the result being a kind of burlesque of 'refined' speech. In *Manservant and Maidservant* the cook tells her guest in the servants hall, on the subject of weak or strong tea: 'My bias is towards the mean . . . I am not in favour of excess in any direction.'

I was up in London during the summer and autumn of 1968, and I was often at Braemar Mansions. She was wonderfully well during this time, and walked as well as she ever would walk. Her sisters were at the club in October, and they told me Ivy had been made a Companion of Honour. Or I was under the impression they told me this. I wrote to congratulate her, saying I would telephone and arrange for a visit with Mary. But the new postal system was in force whereby if you wanted a letter delivered you put a fivepenny stamp on the envelope, and if you put a fourpenny stamp on you hoped for the best. I had put a fourpenny stamp on, and when I rang Braemar Mansions Ivy herself answered the telephone.

She had not received my letter.

'One doesn't get letters now,' she told me, quite cheerfully. She would like to see me, and hoped I would come to tea. I arranged to go on Mary's day off, and make tea for her.

When I arrived she had received my note.

'But my sister got it wrong,' she said. 'I've been made a Companion of Literature. But even so, it's quite a nice little honour.'

I said indeed it was, and I asked her to tell me about it. And after tea she showed me the certificate, signed by Lord Butler and Lord Birkenhead, the Presidents. There was a short, beautifully worded 'testimony' to 'her excellent writing'.

We studied it together. Ivy was obviously touched by this new tribute. She asked me to go to the cupboard in the dining-room where I would find her other honours, her D.B.E. and her C.B.E.

I brought them to her, and we spread them all out, and stared and admired and touched. The D.B.E. was a beautiful decoration. Such quiet moments with Ivy are most precious to remember now. She was in her eighty-fifth year and had written and published nineteen novels, (counting *Dolores*), one of which, *Mother and Son*, had won the James Tait Black Award. She had become an acknowledged classic of our time, not a popular author, but acclaimed for her 'excellent writing'.

When we had put the decorations back in their cases, I told her I would arrange the flowers I had brought. Ivy had an idea by now that flowers kept much better if put on the floor. They got more air, she told me. There were three of her horrible chimney-like vases in a row on the floor, and she asked me to put mine with those. I always longed to give her different vases, but was afraid of hurting her. In some ways she seemed to have no artistic interest in her surroundings. On the other hand she had a special feeling and love for flowers. Her sister, Vera Compton-Burnett told me that as a little girl Ivy had loved flowers, and would amuse the younger children by making little figures from flowers – stalks for arms and legs, petals and leaves for clothes, choosing particular flower shapes for faces. She certainly never lost her love for flowers, but their arrangement was best left to chance, and anyway was irrelevant.

'Flowers are lovely, just as they are,' she would tell me, when I asked, sometimes, if she would mind my giving a vase of flowers a few little tweaks and uplifts here and there. It was a time when most of us had caught the craze for Flower Arrangement, one of the quirks of modern times, Ivy thought it, like frozen foods and wigs. So she watched me in silence when I added my vase of flowers to her row of three. I tried to make a design of the four vases, mixing the colours, taking a flower from one vase and putting it in another, the tall vases at the back, the smaller ones in front to hide those ugly chimney-pots. I thought the result quite pleasing. I had been chatting away to Ivy as I worked, talking about the different flowers – 'Dark flowers must go low in the vase, Ivy, you see, and white ones high, otherwise you get a top-heavy look –' and so on, all of which Ivy digested in silence.

When I had finished and we looked at the result, Ivy said, in her quiet way: 'I liked them in a row.'

I broke into mirth, and of course I put the vases in a row. I thought of this a few weeks after her death, sadly, when I was taking part in a county show of flower arrangement. Walking about the huge marquee, looking at the many original entries depicting 'Any Book Title', my eye caught a book with a yellow jacket entitled *The Present and the Past*. It was Ivy's novel set between different flower arrangements, old and modern. What would Ivy have thought about that, I wondered?

'Snapdragons have grown so large, they look as if they might eat you,' Ivy declared, when I told her that at a recent flower show in Vincent Square I was almost horrified by the size of the delphiniums some of which must have been five feet tall.

As Ivy had not left her flat except to be taken to hospital since she broke her hip in 1965 she was unaware of the more startling changes in the London scene. She had never seen a crowd of young 'Hippies' with their long hair and strange clothes, for instance; she knew of changes only as they affected her way of life, like frozen food – ('Even chickens are frozen! Why is it?').

If I described the London scene to her, she was silent and when I told her that there seemed to be more coloured people every time I came to London, she looked shocked. She said, rather stiffly: 'Doesn't that depend on what part of London you are in?'

It was a question, but it was also a statement, and I let the subject drop. We soon talked about the books we had been reading. I said I had enjoyed Iris Murdoch's new novel *Bruno's Dream*. I said I liked her sentences, one especially: 'Sleep came like an anxious cloud trailing its overtensed knotted limbs.' Not an 'Ivyish' sentence. But in judging a novel Ivy was always more concerned with its structure than with its sentences. And so she pronounced on *Bruno's Dream:* 'It's definitely not good as a novel,' she said. 'Definitely not good.'

This was also a statement, and justified from Ivy's point of view. In all our talks about books she insisted that a novelist must use a plot, a well-shaped plot, with all its parts related, like the bones of a skeleton.

I had always admired Muriel Spark's writing, and Ivy had liked some of her earlier novels, *Momento Mori* in particular. I had not yet read her new book *The Image* and mentioned this to Ivy.

'Well, *don't* read it,' she said, with emphasis. 'It's about *film* people . . . !'

This was a snob barrier, quite typical, and one that brooked of no argument.

5

Ivy died on 27 August 1969. The summer of her death was lovely, a summer that lasted till November.

I was up on 1 June to help at the club, and sent my usual note to Ivy telling her I was in town, and would love to see her, and I would telephone to ask when I could come. And, as always when I first came to London, I rushed about seeing this and that – two flower shows, an exhibition of frescoes from Florence at the Hayward Gallery, and Leonardo's drawings in the Queen's Gallery. I remember I bought two postcards of the drawings to show Ivy.

She answered the telephone herself and I held on while she fetched her diary; I was asked to tea on the following Thursday.

'Mary will be off for a few hours,' Ivy said, 'and I know you don't mind making tea.'

There were peaches in the shops, a fruit Ivy loved, so I took those instead of flowers. Walking down Cornwall Gardens, that corner of London that I thought could never change, I noticed, with horror, scaffolding opposite Braemar Mansions. When I drew closer, builders appeared to be building up from the two-floor block of flats facing the Mansions.

Ivy was sitting before the open balcony window looking out on her little bright garden. She was in a light grey summer dress. I had never seen her in a summer dress before. She looked very small in her armchair.

I stood by her side. 'You can't see that horrible building from here; that's one blessing.'

'Oh, don't talk to me about that building,' she wailed. 'At least it isn't opposite this room. They are putting two floors on top of the block of flats that's there already. My landlord says the man who's doing it is a rogue, but he's been given planning permission.'

One of Ivy's friends joined us for tea. She had lived in the district for many years and was in the throes of moving to a new flat. There were two trolleys laid for tea in the sitting-room. On one was a very large thermos, and on the other a thermos jug.

'This is our new arrangement when Mary goes out, so you don't have to make the tea, Cicely. A friend gave me the thermos. Will you pour out for us. But pour mine from the jug, will you please?'

I had learnt how to pour out tea for Ivy by now. The first time I helped her I put the milk in first because that is how I serve myself. But it was wrong for Ivy. I had to give her a clean cup. Then I poured, leaving room for the milk.

'I like my cup to be filled. I don't like half a cup,' she told me, handing it back to me.

The friend talked of her new flat and the chores of moving and packing. When I turned to Ivy to include her in the conversation I was horrified to see her with her eyes closed, her mouth open, looking pale and small and seemingly unconscious, a piece of toast in her hand.

'She's gone off,' the friend said cheerfully. 'This happens now.'

I said we had better go on talking or the sudden silence would wake her. Our voices lulled her. But suddenly Ivy said:

'That house opposite will be *horrible*!'

It was a wail of distress. Tea went on, and our talk. Ivy had more tea and another small piece of toast. She loved toast.

'Whatever do you want with six rooms?' she asked.

'Well, there's my furniture,' the friend explained. 'It's got to go somewhere. How many rooms have you got?'

I began to count the rooms in Ivy's flat.

'Oh, she's gone again!' the friend said.

Ivy had indeed 'gone' again. This time her arms were raised so that her sleeves fell back and, I think, made her cooler. It was a very hot day. She looked so frail and small, her arms so pitifully thin, I could hardly speak. But I managed to say: 'Well, dining-room, sitting-room, three bedrooms, that's five already. Then there's the kitchen, and the usual offices.'

'Do have some more tea?' Ivy said, waking up suddenly.

She was off once more while we talked, and woke up as suddenly.

'Can one of you find me a dentist?' she said. 'Cicely, can you? My plate is broken, and I have difficulty when I eat. If you could find one who would come to me, I would be so grateful.'

It was something of a Mad Hatter's tea-party. I said:

'Oh, of course, Ivy. I'll do that this evening,' before she fell asleep.

Her friend had to go early, having a lot to do. Ivy asked me to stay on. She fell asleep again and I put the tea things together and wheeled the trolleys out. When I came back Ivy was awake, her walking aid in front of her.

'Let's sit by the window,' she said.

As I helped her from her chair – one was not allowed to give her too much help – I noticed a sort of hump behind her left shoulder. When she stood up and pushed her aid in front of her the cause of it was plain. She was too small and her shoulders were hunched when she gripped her aid, and evidently she put more weight on one arm.

We sat by the window and admired her garden. She sat with her arms above her head, dropping off sometimes. When she woke she rubbed an arm as though it irritated.

'It's been a very hot day, Ivy,' I said. 'And rather tiring for you, I'm sure. I won't stay and tire you more.'

'You don't tire me. I weeded yesterday; I did too much really,' she said. 'It made me tired. And the night *is* so long. I don't sleep now.'

'Do you ever take tablets to help you to sleep?'

'Oh *no* . . . do you?'

Her quick 'do you?' was typical. I remember a journalist asked her once if she had a television. Her reply was: 'No. Have you?'

We both said disapproving things about sleeping tablets. But she was plainly exhausted. I was certain as I watched her, her disfigured shoulder, her thin arms, her frailty and her weariness, that she could not live much longer. She was too tired.

I asked if I could type what she had written of her novel.

'When you see it typed it will help you,' I said.

Ivy gave a moan. 'It will be a terrible manuscript. So much crossed out. It's in such a mess.'

'I don't mind the mess. I know your work so well. I can sort it all out. And if it is in a mess, we should do it together, a little at a time. A mess makes you tired.'

'Yes, it does. But I must finish it first.'

So I left it. I said: 'Well, Ivy, you must. And I'll be ready to help you.'

Having settled the matter she fell asleep.

When Mary came back I said I would have to go. And I promised to find her a dentist.

'Let's make a time for you to come again,' she said. 'Pass me that box.'

This was a cardboard box that held together the few things she used during the day, pencils and pens, her diary and address book and other odds and ends. She put my name down for tea for the following week, and we kissed each other goodbye.

I soon saw a dentist's plate in the Gloucester Road, and a young man in a white coat promised to go the following Monday at six, and the secretary took down the particulars. I went back to Braemar Mansions to let Mary know, and we both went to see Ivy to find out if the time was convenient. It was, and the diary came out again and the appointment entered.

Soon after my visit I met her sister Vera at the club. I told her how much my last visit to Ivy had distressed me. She said Ivy had just had her eighty-fifth birthday and she was sure, as I was, that she couldn't live much longer.

'We had tea together,' she told me, 'and our talk was all of early days, of the birth of another little brother. I asked her if she was writing and she told me she had no time. Yet we took two hours over tea. . . .'

She had noticed her shoulder, but of course had not mentioned it to Ivy. And the irritation was much worse on some days. Poor Ivy! It was too much to suffer all at the same time, and we were both sure she couldn't suffer it much longer.

As Ivy was so weak I hesitated about going again and decided to telephone Mary and find out how things were. Mary told me that 'Dame' was expecting me and I mustn't disappoint her. And she wanted me to make tea for her, and she would go off for an hour or two. This scheme worked very well, and I was able to do this until Ivy died. One got the key from the landlord on the ground floor, and while the kettle boiled I could do a bit of watering.

On my last visit, about a week before she died, I found her sitting in her usual place in the sitting-room, a blue exercise book before her, a pencil in her hand.

I said: 'Oh, Ivy, how marvellous . . . !'

She smiled. 'It's page one. I was just reading what I had written.'

It was very hot, really too hot, I thought, but Ivy this time seemed not at all distressed or exhausted. And tea was normal – 'You make good tea,' she told me, to my huge relief – and we had it in the dining-room. Ivy told me her friend Francis King was threatened with a libel case for something he had written. She wasn't sure about the details and had asked him to come along, but he had a sore throat. She had lost one of her ear-rings – they were valued at £200. But later she found it caught in her dress.

'All my jewellery was stolen when the flat was burgled. My ear-rings are about all I have,' she said.

A great friend had died – Theodora Benson. 'It's been an awful year,' she said. 'One friend dying after another. One feels so lonely.'

She spoke again of her long friendship with Margaret Jourdain. 'We were together for over thirty years.'

I said such a friendship, lasting so long, was rare. She agreed it was rare. 'And wonderful,' she added. 'How I've missed her.'

Then somehow, on that last afternoon together, we talked about saucepans and kitchen equipment. I slipped out to the kitchen for something she wanted, and Ivy quoted Mary:

'Miss Greig won't be bothered finding things in this kitchen. Not like it was in my last place.'

I asked what Mary had meant. Ivy said in her last place the kitchen was full of gadgets. Mary couldn't cope with them, and so she left. Ivy wasn't sure about the gadgets. 'Have you got them?' she asked me.

'Oh, one or two, Ivy. People give them as presents, you know. On the whole they help. They save time.'

Ivy wanted details. 'Well, we've got a timer, a sort of clock thing. If you want your pie or your cake to come out of the oven at twelve o'clock, then you switch the hands to twelve and the alarm goes off at that time. I take it out in the garden with me, and when the alarm goes off I go in and take the cake out of the oven.'

Ivy listened with great interest. 'What else have you got?'

'Someone gave us a pressure-cooker. That's marvellous if you want to cook something quickly.' I told her about pressure cookers.

Ivy said: 'If these things are really so good, then why don't people have them?'

I said: 'Some people do have them. Some people go in for gadgets just because they are gadgets – things like those alarm clocks that wake you up in the morning and make you a cup of tea at the same time.'

Ivy was amused and wholly disbelieving.

'What else?' she asked, wondering perhaps how far I was prepared to go.

124

'Oh well, a friend of mine has an electric mixer – she wouldn't be without it.'

'What does that do?'

'It mixes,' I said, disappointed that I couldn't make wilder claims for it. 'You know, it saves you all that beating with a wooden spoon.'

Ivy clearly didn't know, but she invited me to go on. Rotisseries, liquidisers, potato peelers. . . . I was getting bored. But not Ivy. However, I stopped.

'Why are we talking about gadgets?' I said, laughing.

Ivy said: 'Well, if these things really do what you say, then why doesn't everyone have them?'

So I gave up. Gadgets were putting a kind of gulf between us, like a foreign language. I said they were very expensive anyway, and then they went wrong and had to be taken back to the shop, and perhaps the good old ways of doing things were best really.

I said goodbye to her a little later, and she asked me: why did I have to go? It was half-past six; I told her a friend was calling for me at the club soon after seven, and we were going to have supper together.

Mary had come back. I told Ivy I would come again when Mary went out, and make tea for her. I would arrange with Mary to telephone me. We left it like that, and I went, pleased that Ivy had been her old, alert self, enjoying her tea, quite unlike the exhausted person she had been a week ago.

Some days later I went to the television room at the club to hear the news, and suddenly Ivy's face was on the screen, and the announcer was telling us she had died that morning. It was Wednesday, 27 August.

The news of her death was a shock though we all knew she could hardly live through the summer. London without Ivy seemed unthinkable. For the first days I reproached myself bitterly for not having gone to her when I was in town and might have gone; for not having discussed this or that with her; for not confiding in her more, discussing old family troubles with someone who thrived on them. Family life was Ivy's book; she knew it by heart.

But I was as I was, alas. 'Remorse,' says Sir Ransome in *Two Worlds and their Ways*, 'is the result of a change of mood, not a change of nature.' Ivy was right, as always.

What we miss most, I think, is a unique personality. Because this is, on the whole, a drab age, this quality of uniqueness was something one experienced the moment one met her. It was apt to paralyse one, it often paralysed me.

The next morning Mary rang me, distraught. I promised I would go to her, but she must tell me when the coast was clear. I didn't want to go when lawyers, executors and valuers were there.

'They're here now,' Mary told me. 'But *please* come. The lawyers will be gone by the time you get here. We can sit in the kitchen.'

I reflected that the flat would be more or less over-run by officials for some days, and I promised Mary I would come at once.

We sat in the kitchen and drank tea. The lawyers had gone. A valuer from Harrods was in the dining-room, executors were in the sitting-room. The night nurse had asked if she could stay on for one more night; a sad looking girl, she sat silent and watched us.

The door-bell rang and a cheerful woman followed Mary into the kitchen.

'Tea? How lovely! May I join you?'

It was Mrs Arthur Waley.

Mary was in a bitterly reproachful mood.

'But Mary, surely you expected this?' Mrs. Waley said.

'No, oh no!' Mary cried. 'And it's the way you all knew Dame was going to die and never thought to tell me!'

We tried to comfort her, telling her she had done all she could for Dame; she really, we said, could not have done more.

When Ivy died Mary had summoned friends who lived near. Ivy had died at nine o'clock in the morning. Stephen Pasmore, her doctor, was in hospital as a patient himself at the time, and his partner had been summoned. Her friends, when they arrived, were shocked to see Ivy's face disfigured by a black eye. It was a strange thing to see, they said, poor Ivy, lifeless, with one black eye. What had happened during the night?

But nothing had happened. Ivy had had these slight, subcutaneous haemorrhages before, caused, I believe, by an anaemic condition.

I was worried about Ivy's last manuscript. When Mary got a trolley ready for the executors I offered to take it into the sitting-room.

They had not found a manuscript. I assured them that it must be somewhere, and I told them what it would look like. I wanted to type it, I said, when it was found. They promised they would let me know.

The funeral was to take place on the following Tuesday, 2 Sep-

126

tember. I said I would go with Mary. In the end we both went with Mrs George Orwell.

The gardens at Putney Vale are beautifully laid out. Our flowers to Ivy made a solid bank of brilliant colours by the little chapel. The service could hardly have been briefer, and only the moment when the coffin – such a small coffin – slid slowly from view, brought anguish.

When we returned to Braemar Mansions the familiar sitting-room, always so quiet, was in some confusion. But Ivy's publisher told me the last manuscript had been found and had been taken by Elizabeth Sprigge for safe keeping. I sought her out, and we fixed a time for the following Friday for me to call at her flat.

This was all I wanted to know, and I went to the kitchen to say goodbye to Mary.

'I'm glad I fought to save Dame's life,' she told me, still distraught.

'Yes, Mary, you were wonderful. Did Dame say anything, at the end? Do you remember anything she said?'

Mary said no, not in the morning. Dame had been quiet.

'You don't remember anything she said?'

'I remember what she said the night before she died.'

'What did she say?'

'I asked her, last thing, before I went to bed, if she would like me to make her a hot drink. I knew she was awake.'

'What did she say?'

'She just said: "Leave me alone." That's all she said to me. "Leave me alone." '

6

On the following Friday I called on Elizabeth Sprigge. She had just finished reading as much as she could of that last, disordered manuscript.

She said: 'The last shall be first, and the first last,' one of Ivy's last sentences.

Without saying so we both thought it might make a good title.

I left London the following day, and once I was home I set to work to study the manuscript, carefully, page by page, book by book. There were thirteen or fourteen books, and Ivy had numbered them up to eleven. There was no twelve: the book after eleven was marked NEXT! – exclamation mark and all. There were many pages missing, and many loose pages. My task was to sort it all out and piece it together before I started typing it.

Ivy, fortunately, had two handwritings, the large, sloping scrawl with Greek E's of her letters and postcards, and the small, neat, more upright hand with ordinary e's she used with a pencil when writing her novels. One was relaxed, undisciplined, the other simple and ordered, clear and clean. As long as I knew her she kept these two hands apart, each having a different purpose. But in this manuscript there were the two hands, and it was quite obvious that the scrawling hand belonged to the time when she was frail and exhausted and near the end of her life.

I found that if I read the neatly written version straight through to the last page of the twelfth or thirteenth book, not quite a simple thing to do as many pages were loose and unnumbered, I could make out a straightforward story with a happy ending.

It opens with the usual breakfast scene. Lady Heriot, or Eliza, an intelligent and likeable tyrant, is with her family. She is the second wife of Sir Robert Heriot. She has two stepdaughters, Hermia and Madeline, and two children by her marriage to Sir Robert, Angus and Roberta.

'What an unbecoming light this is,' said Eliza Heriot, looking round from the globe above the table to the faces round it.

'Are we expected to agree?' said her son, as the light fell on her own face. 'Or is it a moment for silence?'

Eliza rules the house and the family; she enjoys power. Her son Angus tells her: 'You might be a figure in history corrupted by power. It is what you are, except that you are not in history.'

Eliza answers: 'It is a pity I am not. It is where I ought to be. I should do a great deal of good.'

Hermia rebels and makes plans to leave home. She decides to help with the management of a large girls' school in the town, her father helping her to buy a partnership. The school has not prospered and Hermia believes, with her ideas for reform and improvement, she can save it. She is the heroine of the novel, she is almost a Brontë or a Jane Austen heroine. At the school concert, which is also Parents Day, she meets a wealthy, middle-aged man, uncle of one of the girls. It is their first and last meeting. He writes, proposing marriage. She refuses by return of post, quite against the wishes of Eliza who sees Hermia's chances of marriage at thirty-four as slight. Soon after, her father finds himself in financial difficulties. Eliza decides they must pack up and live in the dower house, the house at the gates which the servants call the lodge. The big house will be let. While discussions proceed the house-keeper, one of Ivy's most amusing and sharply drawn servants, enters to tell her ladyship that some news 'has emerged'. It is that Mr Grimstone has died. He is the wealthy neighbour, son of Jocasta Grimstone, uncle to Jocasta's grandchildren, and Hermia's rejected admirer. The two houses are on calling terms and the young people have become friends.

Minutes later Mrs Duff comes once more to the assembled family: more news has emerged her ladyship 'would wish to be apprised of'. Mr Grimstone has left all his fortune 'to a strange young lady'. Mrs Duff refuses to divulge more, and the family are left on tenterhooks. News in Ivy's novels always travels via the servants. Or the postman lets fall a word 'while pausing for a cup of tea', or the carpenter, called to mend the backstaircase down which the under housemaid has fallen, breakfasts at the other house, and reports in full.

Mrs Duff soon returns with further news: Mr Grimstone's heiress is Hermia.

Hermia returns home, her attempts at reform having fallen on stony ground. She finds herself the heroine, saviour of the family fortunes. She is cool, generous and businesslike. She returns half the fortune to the Grimstones, and Osbert, Jocasta's grandson, proposes marriage in a letter which Eliza intercepts, reads and hides. It is discovered when both families are together in the Heriot's house and paper is needed for a party game. Eliza is unpredictable, moved to strange moods more from the strength of her love for her husband and her two children than from malice. Once the letter is discovered, and Osbert and Hermia claim each other, she is all warmth, with a mother's joy in a daughter's engagement. It is Osbert who says, of Hermia and himself: 'How the last shall be first, and the first last.'

This outline of the story was mostly written in Ivy's neat, small writing. There was much revision. She had crossed out two or three pages describing a visit of Jocasta to Eliza, though the fact of the visit is left. The talk between the two women was without Ivy's usual sting. Both women were tyrants in their own homes with plenty of sting to their talk, face to face they were concerned with civilities. Ivy put a line across the pages. But when Jocasta is at home, and mourns for her dead son, contrasting his virtues: 'Feeling and sympathy' with her grandchildren who are 'literal, dry and hard', Ivy has crossed out the allusion to the young people: the words are too harsh for a grandmother.

The story as it stands must have seemed altogether too simple a story to Ivy. In 1968 when she wrote telling me she was 'getting back into a little book . . .' she must have tried to fill out the book by introducing one or two sub-plots. But 1968 was too late. Her attempts to introduce more sensational incidents – Jocasta's youngest granddaughter being caught reading the butler's books, for instance, and Roberta announcing that she will marry the man Hermia has rejected – these were written in the frail, exhausted scrawl of her last years. Nothing leads up to these incidents, and they are not developed, so I left them out.

There are some good things in it. Miss Murdoch, the headmistress whom Hermia tries to help, is brilliantly drawn. The paper game played by the two families is amusing and true to life. Eliza's sharp comments on anything that hints of sentiment where the 'working class' is concerned are 'Ivyish' both in style and to the life. Madeline, the dutiful daughter reminds her mother that servants have feelings. She says:

> There is a word to remember through all the easy talk . . . the people we depend on have the same feelings as we have ourselves.'

'How can we remember it when they have quite different ones,' said Eliza.

And when Madeline tries to reason with Hermia whom Eliza finds difficult:

'It may be that tact and patience are needed' (she says), Hermia replies with one of those rhythmic sentences that is not vintage Ivy, however. The rhythm is there but nothing much besides. The charge has gone.

> I told myself that, as everyone would. And I found they did nothing, as everyone does. The decline will go on as nothing is done to check it. A deadlock has been reached, and is not resolved. I am here for the break to achieve it. Though where my presence failed, it is unlikely that my absence will succeed.

So far as it goes, Ivy's last novel is a happy story in which the young of the two families triumph because, on the whole, as in a tale by Jane Austen, good sense prevails.

> If the compulsions of our life were lifted, I wonder what would break forth. . . .

Roberta says. The remark could be taken as a fair comment on Ivy's eighteen novels: they provide the answer.

As the novel was short the publishers decided to include two short introductions, one by Charles Burckhardt on its literary merits, and one by Elizabeth Sprigge on how she found the manuscript after Ivy's death. So one of my four carbon copies was sent out to Burkhardt in California, and Elizabeth Sprigge and I set to work on her introduction in her Kensington flat. My contribution was simply to supply the dates, from Ivy's postcards and letters to me, of the different stages of the book's progress.

We worked well together, and Elizabeth brought it to an end – bar the last sentence.

'How shall I end?' she asked.

'With a quotation,' I said. 'Ivy knows all the answers.'

But what quotation?

I looked for one in *A God and his Gifts*, in the talk between the two authors, but it was not what we wanted.

We took down this novel and that from her shelves. Then she put a book into my hands saying: 'This will interest you.'

It was Ivy's proof copy of *Dolores* inscribed in her sprawling hand – in ink – *To Noel Compton-Burnett from the Author.*

The first pages, where the reader is addressed in the manner of George Eliot and Charlotte Brontë, is scribbled all over with corrections – in pencil.

As I turned the pages I came to the quotation we were looking for. Dolores has read Mr Claverhouse's last manuscript. He tells her there is nothing good in it . . . 'my time for work was past, and my heart was heavy,' he says. Dolores answers:

> 'There is great good in it', said Dolores, turning the pages with grave scrutiny. 'You must give yourself to it again, and carry it on to its end. It is not like the work of your prime; but then it is not the work of your prime. It will have its own value for that.'

We had both thought of Osbert's phrase 'How the last shall be first and the first last,' as a good title. Ivy gave the story no title herself and no hint of what it might be. Osbert's phrase was used more than once by Ivy. It comes in *The Mighty and their Fall*, and in *A God and his Gifts* and in *A Father and his Fate*. The title had to have the familiar rhythm, and have a bearing on the story. I thought also of Mr. Firebrace's speech in *Two Worlds and their Ways*. He has seen a son of his for the first time, an illegitimate son. For family reasons it must be the last time, as well as the first. I read the words again after Ivy's death, and heard her own, quiet voice in them. They can be her last words here.

> 'The first and the last. My hail and farewell. *My ave atque vale*. Well, we will leave it so. I have sent my message, sent my token across the years, seen – well, that is enough. I will be content.'

Index